MW01109242

MASTER OF NONE

A LOVE/HATE AFFAIR WITH HOME REMODELING

By

Jerry R. Davis

MONTAÑAS PRESS

2820 MONUMENT DR. NW
ALBUQUERQUE, NEW MEXICO

ISBN: 978-1-933582-42-9

Credits:
Cover artist: Jinger Heaston

Printed in the United States of America

Dedication

I would like to dedicate this book to all the home remodeling do-it-yourself individuals somewhere out there in the world. They probably will recognize themselves in these pages and will be able to identify with the situations described.

Acknowledgements

I wish to thank all the people who made this book possible. My critique group (The Untitled Critiquers) made up of Sabra Steinsiek, Kate Harrington, Mary Lombardo, Beverly Eschberger and Pat Gonzales suffered through the reading of each chapter and made many valuable corrections and suggestions. Later, they proofread the entire manuscript.

I am indebted to Ron Baldwin, Stephen Vat, Jr. and many others for supplying information when my own memory failed me.

Three organizations, SouthWest Writers, the New Mexico Book Co-op and Writers to Writers Workshop provided me with valuable training in the art of writing, needed technical and publishing information and constant support for which I am most grateful.

Other Books By

Jerry R. Davis

Home On The Farm

Tales Of The Road

Leafing Through My Family Tree

TABLE OF CONTENTS

Apartments & Homes Where I Have Lived (1955 – 2008)

1955 – 1955 - Abbott Rd. Apartment (Lansing, MI)

1955 – 1956 - Cass Ave. Apartment (Vassar, MI)

1956 – 1958 - Army Barracks (Ft. Leonard Wood, MO, Ft. Lee, VA, Ft. Jackson, SC)

1958 – 1959 - Frank St. Apartment (Caro, MI)

1959 – 1961 - Main St. Apartment (Vassar, MI)

1961 – 1961 - Genesee Ave. Apartment (Saginaw, MI)

1961 – 1962 - Jefferson Ave. Apartment (Saginaw, MI)

1962 – 1964 - Whittier St. House (Saginaw, MI)

1964 – 1965 - Federal Ave. Apartment (Saginaw, MI)

1965 – 1967 - Whittier St. House (Saginaw, MI)

1967 – 1972 - Brockway St. House (Saginaw, MI)

1972 – 1975- Center Rd. Apartment (Saginaw, MI)

1975 – 1979 - Lake James House (Prudenville, MI)

1979 – 1979 - Bayliss St. Apartment (Midland, MI)

1979 – 1984 - Campbell Ct. House (Midland, MI)

1984 – 1997 - Sinclair St. House (Midland, MI)

1997 – 2008 – Monument Dr. House (Albuquerque, NM)

Prologue

I have been an adult for approximately five and a half decades and have lived in fifteen different residences in seven cities since permanently moving away from my parents' home. Nine of those fifteen residences were rental apartments, from small to large, and six of them were houses that I owned. I have never lived in a *rental house*—only rental apartments or self-owned houses.

Several residences are missing from the above listing. They are the three different military barracks I lived in during the two years while I was a guest of the United States Army. Though the barracks left much to be desired as ideal places to live, I never had the temerity to make any changes in them. Surely that would have been frowned upon by the military powers that were. The first of the barracks was at Ft. Leonard Wood, Missouri, where I was subjected to the eight weeks of infantry basic training. That military post soon became my least favorite place on earth. The summer heat and humidity were nearly unbearable, the training was rigorous, especially for someone like me who viewed exercise and sports with disdain. The animal life, which included both venomous snakes and venomous spiders, was frightening. We trainees had a favorite saying, "If God were going to give the world an enema, we knew where he would stick it—Ft. Leonard Wood."

The infantry trainees, in general, lived in open barracks. They were very large dormitories with a row of double decked cots on either side. There was only one bathroom per barrack and it contained toilets, urinals and showers with no cubicles and no window coverings. Privacy was nonexistent. My living situation was a trifle better as I was one of four squad leaders in my training company and, therefore, was assigned to half of what is called a "cadre" room. At the ends of the barracks were two rooms on each floor where the non- commissioned officers (cadre leaders) were assigned. I shared one of those rooms with another of the squad leaders from our company. Though it was small, the room did provide a modicum of privacy. The barracks accommodations at my other military assignments—Ft. Lee, Virginia and Ft. Jackson, South Carolina—were about the same. They were serviceable but totally without decorative merit or any real comfort. During those two army years, it was necessary for me to hold my renovation impulses in abeyance.

All fifteen of my other dwelling places, including the present one, whether apartments or houses, have become the objects of my persistent preoccupation with remodeling. I must confess that I never moved into a residence, or even visited one, which I felt was perfect. All of them, in my estimation, were in dire need of my invaluable help in making them more attractive, homier or more practical places in which to live. So it follows that, even today, when I find myself in a home or apartment, whether as a guest or an inhabitant, invariably I am overtaken with a strong urge to tear out a wall, move a doorway, repaint a room, put up different window coverings, replace the artwork on the walls, or at the very least re-arrange the furniture. Once in a while I have displayed overzealous candor and even made suggestions to home owners. Some of those "helpful hints" were accepted with good grace and some were viewed with contempt. The latter were obvious and I could see by the people's expressions that they were asking themselves, "Who is he to give me advice about my own home?" Fortunately, most of my Good Samaritan suggestions were merely ignored. Alas, no one really likes a do-gooder, no matter how pure his or her intentions.

This volume is designed to take the reader on an entertaining and irreverent gambol through my life of home renovation starting at the tender age of ten. As is true with William Shakespeare's plays, some of my stories are tragedies, though none were fatal, and some are comedies. It is my hope that each of the vignettes will be enjoyed by one and all and that they will give rise to a few chuckles over the situations that I describe. In this way you can share my very own "magnificent obsession" with remodeling and renovating.

Jerry R. Davis
Albuquerque, New Mexico – 2009

Chapter One

Baby Steps In Renovation

Interest in building and remodeling came down to me through my mother's side of the family. Mother's grandfather, Abraham Williamson, was a handyman and carpenter during much of his life. Her father, Jacob Franklin Williamson, was at various times in his professional career, a carpenter as well as a designer and builder of fine furniture. Also, in order to adequately house his eleven children, Grandfather Williamson spent many years remodeling the family's four-room one-story house into a two-story eight-room residence which dominated the street where it was situated.

Some of my earliest memories involve watching my mother poring over house remodeling plans. Therefore I, too, could read a basic house plan and recognize a drawing of the exterior elevation of a house from an early age. When I was only six or seven years old, Mother entered a contest sponsored by the *Better Homes and Gardens* magazine. The contestants were assigned the task of remodeling their own homes on paper. Our house was a nearly one hundred year old Greek Revival style house similar to many others on Michigan farms. Few renovations had taken place since it was built; therefore amenities like running water, a bathroom and central heating were missing. In the magazine contest the participants were required to include before and after floor plans, interior and exterior drawings as well as landscape designs. I was fascinated watching Mother make the necessary drawings and often we compared notes about what alterations she should make to improve the farmhouse. Perhaps some of my suggestions even helped her win the fifty dollar Honorable Mention prize.

Another of Mother's building projects on the farm where I was born involved chickens. When Dad bought baby chicks in the early spring of each year, they were housed, for warmth, in our kitchen during their first few weeks of life. Mother objected to that and set about constructing a coop for them. However, before the building was finished, we moved. I was nine years old when Dad and Mother sold the Tuscola farm and bought a much larger one near the small city of Vassar. Though the move to the larger community was only five miles in distance, it made a tremendous difference in our lives both socially and economically.

The Vassar house was equally as unsatisfactory comfort-wise as the Tuscola one had been. Consequently Mother began to make changes in it almost immediately. For example, she drew plans for and built closets in each of the two first-floor bedrooms as there had been none previously. It seemed as though no home building feat was beyond Mother's scope. I thoroughly enjoyed watching each of her projects develop from planning to completion and I learned much from them and from her.

I drew my own first house floor plan when I was ten years old and in the sixth grade. Each day after completing my assigned school work I usually had a few minutes left before it was time to go home. On that particular occasion I remember getting out my notebook and making an extremely rough drawing of a one-story house. It had four rooms—a living room, a kitchen and two bedrooms (we had no bathroom in our own home, so I didn't include one in mine either). I completed the plan by carefully drawing furniture in each of the rooms and then took it home to show it to Mother. She attempted to hide the little smile which crossed her face while looking at my "masterpiece." Then she explained in a gentle and supportive way that the drawing was very nice but, there was no door leading to the outside. Mother went on to add that people could easily move from room to room through doorways I had included, but they would be unable to go in and out of the house except through the windows. I was chagrined and vowed to do better with the next attempt.

When I reached my middle teens and was in high school, I began to victimize our farmhouse with my renovation fervor. The first of those projects I can remember involved masonry. At the rear of the house was a large cement terrace or patio area with three or four steps at its far side leading down to the driveway. Where the patio joined the house, both the supporting wall and the house foundation had deteriorated. In fact one could look directly into the basement through a small hole in the foundation where a half dozen bricks had fallen away. Though I had never done any cement work previously, I decided to try my hand at a repair job.

First, I started with the house foundation. I removed the loose bricks around the opening and then mixed some mortar in an old wash tub. Then I re-mortared the bricks into their correct places again. All went well and when I was finished that corner of the house was once again being supported by a solid foundation. So far, so good, I thought.

Though I had gained some confidence with the success of my first masonry job, I still viewed the repair of the patio foundation with trepidation. A four-foot section of the wall supporting the patio had collapsed over the years. Broken pieces of cement lay where they had fallen. First I dragged the pieces away and threw them in the gully behind the corncrib so that I could view the situation better. The gaping hole that remained stared back at me malevolently. "How am I going to solve this problem?" I wondered to myself.

At last I was struck by an idea. What if I built a set of cement steps in the gap which would match those at the far end of the patio? They would fit almost perfectly into the four-foot break in the wall and they would provide a handy shortcut for Mother to follow on her frequent trips to the garden. Using scrap lumber I found around the farmstead, I built forms for three steps and then filled them with stones and other debris high enough so they could be topped by about three or four inches of solid cement. I got bags of ready-mixed concrete and once again put the old wash tub to use for mixing it.

Preparations for the project required an enormous amount of work covering several days but eventually I was ready to pour the cement. Because I lacked the proper trowel for working the wet concrete, I used what tools were available to smooth it. Those turned out to be my own hands in work gloves. They seemed to do the job all right, but by the time I was finished, I was in severe pain. When I pulled off my gloves, I saw what the problem was. Liquid concrete had seeped through the porous gloves and saturated my fingers and palms while I was smoothing the steps. Apparently the cement contained lye or some other strong ingredient that actually ate holes in my skin. The concrete granules ground into those open wounds and made them awfully painful. For a few days after that I went about my work around the farm with my hands in bandages while the skin healed. The cement steps, by the way, turned out well and were used for over twenty years. In fact, they were in place until the house was torn down by the next owner of the farm.

When I was in my late teens and only home from college during summer vacations and holiday breaks, I still worked on remodeling the farmhouse. One summer I had a brainstorm which I felt would make the home much more livable. Like most houses constructed in the middle 1800s, originally there were no closets in the bedrooms. My mother had already added them in the two first-floor bedrooms—the one occupied by my sister and the other by Mother and Dad. However, my two brothers and I were relegated to the up-stairs bedrooms where we had to use wall hooks to hang our clothing.

Between the two upstairs bedrooms was a third room, about eight by eight feet in size, which was used for general storage. The room was without windows because it had no exterior walls and it was entered through a doorway from the hall. I came up with the idea of dividing the storage room into three closets—a walk-in closet, about four by six, for each of the two bedrooms and a general storage closet, approximately two by eight feet, off the hallway. I carefully measured the entire second floor and drew a plan of it to scale on graph pa-per. Then I drew a second plan showing the changes I envi-sioned. (See reproductions of the floor plans at the end of this chapter.)

When I approached my parents with the plans in hand, they, of course, had many questions about details of the project. Apparently I was able to answer all of them to their satisfaction because eventually I got the okay to go ahead. With their approval, I happily set to work on the scheme.

Being a true novice, I had little idea how much of a mess was in store for me. I soon learned that sawing through plastered walls results in bushels of debris and inches of dust on every surface. I cut openings for doorways from the two bedrooms into the storage room and a sizeable pile of broken plaster resulted. I framed the resulting openings with new two by fours before turning to the other doorway. After I had doubled its width the pile of dusty plaster also doubled in size. I ignored the ugly behemoth I had created and, instead of attacking the mess, framed the new larger doorway. By that time Mother was complaining about the dust I was causing throughout the rest of the house. Removing the mountain of plaster required lugging two pails at a time on trip after trip, down the stairs, through the dining room and kitchen, out the back door and across the rear yard to a small gully where we always buried our refuse. Next I had to clean the house both upstairs and down. When that gargantuan task was accomplished I could return to the building project.

After I had constructed door jambs for the three added doorways and put them in place, I began building the dividing walls which would carve up the old storage room into the three new closets. I framed the new walls with two by fours and covered them with sheets of wallboard. That part of the project, of course, resulted in more dust accumulation. "Would the clean-up part of the job *never* end?" I wondered.

At that point the three closets were in place but only in a "roughed in" shape. If I were doing that project today, my next step would be to use two coats of plaster or "mud," as it is called, to smooth the joints between the sheets of wallboard. However, up to then I had never had any experience with plaster. I only knew that it made a frightful mess when it was applied wet and later an even worse one when it was sandpapered smooth. Surely my mother's patience would be tried beyond all normal limits if I brought such chaos into the house.

While searching my brain for an alternative I came up with this. I covered all the wallboard joints with two inch masking tape and then wallpapered the interiors of the three closets. Though the wallpaper covered the joints, it was far from perfect. Nonetheless it was serviceable and required only a minimum of mess. I reasoned, also, that since the walls were hidden inside the closets, their imperfections would not be readily noticeable.

Still another problem arose and I took the easy way out of it—by avoidance. Ideally the closets in the bedrooms should have had hinged doors and the wider hallway closet should have had sliding doors. However, we did not live in a perfect world and I knew full well that I was incapable of hanging doors—either the hinged or the sliding type. That was a building skill that I learned years later. Consequently, the door openings remained uncovered for quite a while. Finally, Mother came up with a practical and workable solution. She attached round wooden rods inside the door jambs and then made curtains that hung from them and covered the openings. I had thought of that idea previously but, alas, I was as incompetent at operating a sewing machine as I was at hanging doors.

My final renovation project for the farmhouse involved making yet another improvement in that second-story bedroom I occupied during my college years. In order to explain, I must digress a bit. My first year at Michigan State depleted practically all of my savings so I decided to stay home and get a job during what would have been my sophomore year. In that way I hoped to accumulate enough money to return the following year. Much of that year I spent in Vassar working at Temple's Electric Shop. My job there was to go out on electrical remodeling projects with one of the other employees and serve as his assistant. The correct term, as I recall, was "electrician's helper."

Working for the electrical shop taught me much about house wiring, most of which I still remember today. In fact, I became confident enough that I undertook the job of rewiring my own bedroom in the farmhouse. When electricity was added to the old house, likely during the 1920s or 1930s, only the very basics were included. My second floor bedroom, for example, had only one porcelain fixture with a single bulb. It was situated on a side wall at about eye level. The fixture had a single plug outlet next to the bulb and both of them were operated by a single pull-chain. That was the extent of the electricity in the entire room and I found it to be inadequate for my needs.

Over the next few weeks I put a new light fixture in the middle of the ceiling which was controlled by a switch beside the door to the hallway. To accomplish that it was necessary to use a key hole saw to cut a hole in the ceiling and another by the door for the switch. Then I squirmed through the small hatchway into the attic above and threaded Romex (a cable containing two strands of insulation-clad wire) to the holes before attaching the wires at the fixture and its switch.

As an additional improvement, I wanted to add a couple of electrical outlets on the north wall of the room. To accomplish that, I needed to locate some nearby electrical source for providing power to them. As an experiment I cut out part of a single flooring board near the wall. Luckily that board hid wires that were a part of the ancient system called "knob and tube" wiring. The system involves bare wires attached to porcelain insulators (knobs) which go through the wooden beams via porcelain cylinders (tubes). After cutting off the electrical power at the fuse box, I soldered the old wires to those in the Romex cable and then threaded it to the new outlets. When the re-wiring was completed I replaced the floorboard and one could barely tell it had been removed.

Because of my previous experience with electric fences for controlling our cattle, I have great respect for the zapping power of electricity. Even today, whenever I do electrical work I become nervous concerning what will happen when I turn the power back on. Will sparks fly? Will I be electrocuted? Will the house go up in flames? Since that bedroom re-wiring job was my first project of that sort, I hesitated for quite a time at the fuse box. When I gained the necessary nerve to screw the fuse in, thankfully nothing unexpected happened. To my great satisfaction the new ceiling light, its switch and the electrical outlets all worked fine. I felt no little amount of pride because I had gained yet one more renovating skill. With each little progression my faltering baby steps in home remodeling became more sure-footed.

CLOSET REMODEL
DAVIS FARM HOUSE - 1848

BEFORE

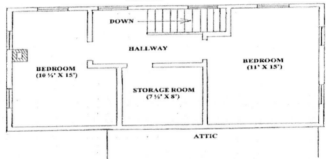

AFTER

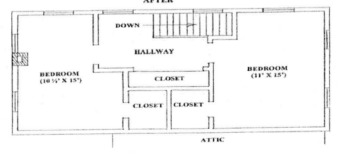

Chapter Two

The Vicarious Remodeler

Sometimes it isn't necessary for the dedicated renovator to actually go through the remodeling process himself
in order to enjoy following the progress of a house reconstruction while it is in process. The only necessary require-
ment is that he must be in the right place at the right time. I
was that fortunate person in 1950 when I was a freshman at
Michigan State University.

During the years 1949 to 1955 while I was earning
my bachelor's degree at MSU, the university went through a
burgeoning growth process. The school's population grew
from a mere twelve thousand students to over twenty thousand in that time, plus its population doubled once again
during the next decade. Those years saw the East Lansing
site flooded with veterans taking advantage of the benefits
of the G.I. Bill of 1945. In addition, a new nation-wide interest in advanced education encouraged thousands of other
students to seek their degrees as well. Consequently building and remodeling projects were progressing on every part

of the campus. New dormitories were built, hundreds of additional classrooms werc addcd, the Student Union Building was tripled in size, a new sports field house rose near the Red Cedar River, the football stadium grew into a full blown bowl, a new library was constructed and, most interesting for me, the President's Home on Circle Drive in the center of the campus was remodeled and enlarged.

The President's Home was just across the street from the Student Union Building and I passed it on my way to and from classes each day. The house was an early Victorian structure with some characteristics of the Spanish Eclectic Revival style. Built in 1857, it was one of the first college buildings erected on the campus. I would guess that the two-story brick structure encompassed roughly three thousand square feet which included a wooden one-story kitchen and utility area at the rear. That year I watched the house evolve into a contemporary style L-shaped mansion at least three times its initial size. It grew into a most suitable venue for serving as not only the personal but the ceremonial home for the president. Clearly, it was designed to be one more indication of the importance Michigan State had attained in recent times.

At the start, I satisfied myself by walking past the remodeling project and observing it from the sidewalk. However, that soon proved totally inadequate for my avid curiosity. I wanted to see it in its entirety which meant viewing it from inside as well as out. The house and grounds became an extremely busy work site during the renovation process. Daily, dozens of trucks and delivery vehicles parked in the yard. Lumber, bricks, shingles and a variety of other building supplies were stacked everywhere. Each day during the work hours the doors throughout the structure remained open while carpenters, plumbers, electricians, architects and engineers scurried in and out like bees around a hive. According to the school newspaper, the university president, Dr. John A. Hannah, and his family had vacated the premises. Therefore, since they were living elsewhere in temporary quarters, there was little danger of my running into or disturbing them while satisfying my curiosity about the project. That was one of the facts that gave me added courage, but it was not the only one.

It was a surprise to me that there was no fence around the work site. I doubt that would be the case today, considering the constant danger of pilfering plus the possibility of accidents affecting workers as well as onlookers. The apparent lack of security spurred me on to further exploration. One day I gathered up my courage and stepped off the front sidewalk and onto the lot. No one gave me a second glance as far as I could tell. Assuming an air that I had important business on the site, I opened my school notebook and pretended to take copious notes as I walked around the entire house peering in all the first floor windows and doors. That tour gave me a much clearer picture of the interior of the house and added to my desire to see even more.

Realizing that discretion was the better part of valor, I decided to take the adventure one step at a time. After all, more had been accomplished on that first visit than I ever dreamed possible, so I went on my way very well satisfied. It wasn't until about two weeks later that I next had an opportunity to visit the remodeling site so my curiosity had to be put on hold while I went about my busy activities around the campus.

Eventually my obsession about the house became nearly overpowering. It was almost as if I were an addict hooked on illicit drugs. The building site drew me back again and again. In fact I was there so often that some of the workmen began to recognize me because they would nod and say hello when they saw me. Apparently they just assumed that I belonged to one of the crews or that I was an architectural student who had been assigned to study the remodeling project. By that time I was snooping everywhere in the house with my trusty notebook and pencil at hand— all the while industriously jotting down imaginary notes. It was utterly fascinating to observe all of the miniscule details of the workmen's techniques as they tripled the size of the home. They accomplished it in such a seamless way that the finished product appeared as though it had always been exactly as it turned out.

Toward the front of the house I found where they kept the detailed architectural drawings for the project. A big stack of them rested on a makeshift table in the entrance hallway where they were constantly referred to by the various workmen. I, too, pored over those plans repeatedly and, in doing so, gained a real sense of what the house was becoming in its reincarnation.

I learned that the first floor of the original part of the house was being divided into two rooms, one of which was a large formal entrance hall with an open stairway. Doors from that hallway led to an enormous living room that had been added on the right. It had a fireplace along its front wall and on the back wall French doors led out to a patio. Beyond the living room on the west was an added sun porch at the end of the house. On the opposite side of the entranceway was a secondary side exit next to a paneled study which contained another fireplace.

Through an arch at the rear of the entrance hall, one could enter the new wing of the house. There a longer hallway led to the formal dining room on the right which, like the living room, had a fireplace and a wall of glass viewing the patio. On the left was a smaller family dining room. Separating the latter from the gigantic kitchen was a butler's pantry/serving area. The hallway ended at the back entrance and also gave access to the multiple garages. There, too, a second stairway led not only to the basement but to the upper level rooms as well.

On the second floor a master bedroom above the living room contained its own *en suite* bathroom, dressing room and walk-in closets. If my memory serves me correctly, four additional family bedrooms, each with its own bathroom, were located above the dining rooms, pantry and kitchen. The space over the garages contained two servants' rooms which shared a bathroom.

Under the entire house, except the garages, there was a full finished basement. Its largest space was taken up with a family room directly below the living room. The balance of the area contained a recreation room, a hobby room, a laundry room, a furnace and utility room, plus a variety of storage areas. All of those were accessed from a hallway covering the entire distance from the formal front stairway to the secondary stair near the back entrance.

My microscopic observation of the home remodeling went on for nearly six months and I would venture to guess that no workman on the site knew the details of the house any better than I came to know them at the time. All good things, however, must come to an end. Thus when the project was nearing completion I was forced to go through a period of withdrawal from it. By that time the work force was diminishing so I began to feel rather conspicuous when I would visit the site. Amazing as it seems though, I was never challenged by anyone on the premises. As sections of the house were completed the workmen began locking those rooms so my areas of observation were severely curtailed. Finally, just a short time before President Hannah and his family moved back into their newly renovated home, I returned to observing the site from the safety of the sidewalk. Thus ended my short career as The Vicarious Remodeler.

A couple of years later, when I was a junior, I took a part time job as a waiter with the catering service of the Student Union Building across the street from the house. Occasionally we were called upon to cater teas, coffee hours and other small gatherings at the President's Home. While serving the guests at those events, I never let on to Miss Lessner, my supervisor, that I knew every nook and cranny in the entire mansion. I felt certain that she, whom I thought of as a vicious martinet, would have been unhappy about it. Miss Lessner regularly made it very clear that we were merely the hired help and must maintain a servile attitude at all times— we should, in a sense, disappear into the woodwork until we were needed. I chuckled secretly about my clandestine past as The Vicarious Remodeler and gloated over the intimate knowledge I had gained about the President's Home while in that guise.

REMODEL OF THE
MICHIGAN STATE UNIVERSITY
PRESIDENT'S HOME
East Lansing, Michigan (1949 – 1950)

BEFORE

Photo Courtesy of
Michigan State University Archives and Historical Collections

AFTER

Photo Courtesy of
Jerry R. Davis

Chapter Three

Apartments Need Renovation Too

Many of the rental apartments I lived in were short-term residences. Though they often were in need of changes to make them more comfortable, I was unwilling to do much to them. Usually those renovations could not be taken with me when I moved, therefore I felt it would be both money and work down the drain. Though I did make some changes to every apartment I lived in, most of them were minor in nature. As examples, I usually re-painted every room, often replaced curtains and draperies and sometimes replaced the hardware on kitchen cupboards. One time I even sanded the hardwood floor of an apartment living room and refinished it. That last however, was an exception to the rule. What follows are additional noteworthy exceptions.

In the fall of 1958 I took a job as a junior high school social studies teacher in a small town, called Caro, near my hometown. While searching for a place to live, I located a three-room apartment in a Queen Anne style Victorian house on Frank Street. The landlord had divided the big old house into four apartments, plus a single room which also was rented out. My apartment was on the first floor and had a kitchen, bathroom and small bedroom, all of which had been added to the original house. The largest space in the unit, the living room, had once been the side parlor of the home. I liked the apartment immediately but, before I signed the rental contract, I knew some dramatic changes had to be made.

The living room had a corner fireplace which I especially liked. The woodwork around the doors, however, was made of dark hardwood carved into a complicated Victorian design. Though all of it was lovely, I felt it was just not very well suited to the style of my furniture. Another problem was that there were far too many openings in the room. They numbered six, including the fireplace, a double pair of pocket doors leading into the landlord's apartment, another door which led to the rental room, a door to the outside, a large window and finally, a doorway to my kitchen. Each side of the room had at least one opening which meant there was no wall area to serve as a background for the sofa or any other piece of furniture.

But, the most vexing issue was the matter of privacy. As the unit existed, the landlord and his wife would have free access to my apartment. Even worse, the tenant in the single room entered his room through my living room! Unbelievable! When I mentioned that problem to the landlady, I recall how surprised she was about my objection. She, obviously, had the typical small town mentality wherein no one locked their doors and anyone could enter or exit from private residences with impunity. That varied greatly from my philosophy and I made that very clear to her. For a while we were at an impasse in our dealings.

To break the deadlock, I asked the landlady if there were some other way the renter could enter his room. She agreed that there was. Eventually I came up with a solution that in my opinion solved all the other problems. We could conquer them by covering both the pocket door and the rental room door with wallboard. But, instead of either screwing or nailing the wallboard in place, we would use masking tape to attach them to the door surrounds; thus saving the beautiful woodwork and hiding it from view. Then by painting the new wallboard the same color as the walls, the doorways would nearly disappear. That also solved the privacy problem because no one could enter my apartment unless they came through the wallboard. Finally, as a bonus, the additional wall space would help with furniture placement. Therefore, the plan satisfied all my issues.

Of course before the plan could be implemented, it was necessary to convince the owners of its feasibility. First I approached the landlady with the idea. Naturally, I had made drawings of the proposal and they seemed to help the cause. My explanation satisfied the landlady well enough that she broached the subject, along with the solution, to her husband. My distinct impression was that he thought I was completely out of my mind, but he was willing to go along with the idiocy if I would agree to do all the work, including the painting. That stipulation was fine with me as it was exactly what I had intended in the first place. Consequently, we signed the rental contract and I was able to go to work on the project.

When the changes were made, the living room turned out to be one of the most pleasant in any of my rentals before or since. (See the plan of the apartment at the end of this chapter.) I was extremely proud to show the place to all of my friends and family who visited me. Even today, when I visit Caro, I always drive by the house in order to remind myself of the good times I had there—during both the renovation time and the short time that I lived there.

After leaving the Caro apartment I moved to another one in my home town of Vassar which was sixteen miles distant from Caro. The unit was on the second floor over a drugstore near the center of the downtown business district. The building's architecture was especially intriguing to me because I felt it was a diamond in the rough just waiting for a person like me, brimming with decorating ideas, to take it in hand.

All the rooms in the apartment, including the bathroom and closet had twelve foot ceilings which I found fascinating. The flat consisted of a large living room on the west with beautiful maple floors. Next to that was a long, narrow kitchen with an eating area at one end. Located behind the living room, the medium sized bedroom contained no windows because it was in the center of the building. An enormous skylight in one corner provided it with natural light. The shaft of the skylight rose an additional ten feet above the bedroom's twelve foot ceiling, thus making the skylight a dramatic twenty-two feet from the floor. Connected to the north side of the bedroom was an antiquated bathroom dominated by an enormous, antique claw-foot bathtub along one of its walls. The flat was a charming living space and I was enthralled with it from the first time I saw it.

One of the few complaints I had about the apartment was that there was no entrance foyer. One entered directly into the living room from a public hallway which also served the two other units on that floor of the building. I pondered the situation for a while and then had an idea which, not only solved the problem nicely, but was also attractive and utilitarian. I built a guest closet in the living room and placed it so it formed a small hallway just inside the entrance door. (See the floor plan and drawing at the end of this chapter.)

The closet was built of three-quarter inch plywood and had a pair of sliding doors on the front. It was sturdy enough that it stood on its own and needed no anchoring. Though it could be moved, the closet was rather heavy. In order to make the addition appear as a permanent fixture, I painted it the same color as the living room walls. The plywood sheets used to make the closet were eight feet tall, thus its top was four feet below the ceiling's twelve foot level. The storage unit's location appealed greatly to my decorative sensibilities because, in the end it actually served three functions—as a wall divider, as additional storage space and as a decorative plant ledge. As an interesting side note about that structure, I lived in the Vassar apartment for somewhat over two years and, at the end of that time, I disassembled the closet and took it with me. Eventually parts of it ended up being used in several of my later renovation projects

It was probably in 1961 that I moved to an apartment on Genesee Avenue in Saginaw, Michigan—a much larger city roughly twenty miles west of my home town. I had accepted a junior high teaching position there and wanted to live near my job. The new apartment was a third floor walkup above an insurance agency not far from the main business district. The building likely was built during the 1920s and it was obvious that the apartments on its second and third floors had little done to them since that time. All the rooms in the flat I rented needed painting, but two areas required much more—the kitchen and the bathroom.

The kitchen was particularly needy and I decided to do a major overhaul there if the building owners would allow it. My justification for the work and expense was that the rent was cheap and I planned to live there for the foreseeable future which might be quite a long time. As it turned out the "quite a long time" was only about a year, but nonetheless I had fun doing the remodeling and at least was able to enjoy the result for that short period of time. As for the owners' permission, it was easily obtained. When I approached them about the changes I wanted to make they gave me *carte blanche* to go ahead. They were obviously very pleased to have a tenant who cared enough about the apartment to do the improvements they had failed to do.

The first eyesore that I tackled in the kitchen was an ugly old gas water heater. It was at least as old as the building and crouched menacingly in a prominent corner of the room. Rising out of its top was a rickety smoke pipe which angled toward a vent in the outside wall. To hide the decrepit appliance I used framing and wallboard and built a cupboard that extended from floor to ceiling. The heater was accessed through a door in the front. Later I painted the cupboard the same as the rest of the kitchen. What an improvement that was. The room looked years younger already.

On the kitchen's north wall hung a giant white porcelain sink with a built-in drain board on either side. The unsightly drain pipe and other plumbing under the sink were all exposed to view, especially from the dining room. That bothered the decorator in me so I built a cupboard under the sink. I fitted out the cupboard with shelves and hung doors on the front. When that was completed and the new cupboard had been painted to match the others, the kitchen began to look like a part of the Twentieth Century.

With those successes under my belt, I turned to the outmoded cupboards and countertops. The upper cupboards extended all the way to the deeper base cupboards so there was very little counter space—in fact, only a few inches. To solve that problem I cut the upper cupboards off about two feet above the lower cabinets and hung smaller doors on the, then, shorter cabinets. Next I covered the counters with red vinyl. The effect was amazing. There was counter space under all the cupboards and, when they were repainted, they looked like modern ones. (See the diagram page at the end of this chapter.)

The bathroom required far less work than the kitchen. The main things it lacked were storage space for towels, a mirror over the sink and a cabinet for tooth brushes, toothpaste, et cetera. I felt like a real veteran after all the cabinetry I had constructed in the kitchen, so I set to work on the smaller project with lots of confidence. Nothing serious got in my way and soon the bathroom was functioning well with a new mirror and the necessary storage areas it had previously lacked.

I spent at least a month on the combined kitchen and bathroom projects but, considering the end result, thought it was time well spent. Needless to say, the owners of the apartment were nearly as pleased with the end product as I was. After all, they gained a nearly new kitchen and a much improved bathroom from the deal. Renovations like those I've described in this chapter were important in my remodeling education. If I had not been able to "cut my teeth" on projects in the apartments, I feel certain that I would never have been willing or able to tackle the much larger undertakings I faced later as a homeowner.

FRANK STREET APARTMENT
CARO, MICHIGAN - 1958

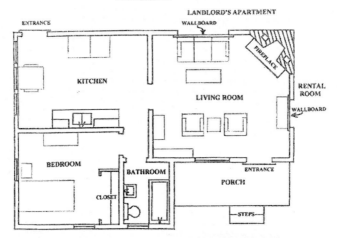

I took this photo in 2008, fifty years after I lived there. The house had gone through many changes for the better in the interim. My apartment was on the right side lower floor. The three connected windows were in my kitchen and the single window was in my bedroom. (See floor plan above.) jrd

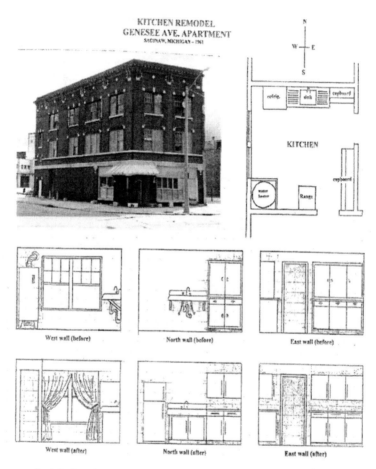

I took the above photo in 2008, forty-seven years after I lived there. The building appeared to be abandoned—note the boarded up windows. My apartment took up the entire third floor and the second bank of two windows on the left led into the kitchen. (See plan and elevations above.) jrd

MAIN STREET APARTMENT
VASSAR, MICHIGAN - 1959

Downtown Vassar – Many
Years before I lived there
(Note the style of autos)

Living Room with new
Closet in place

Chapter Four

Finally, I Renovate My *Own* Home!

I was discharged from the army in1958 and for the next three plus years I lived in four different apartments. It seemed that I was spending my money and time mainly for various landlords' gain and not for my own. Since that situation was beginning to pall, I decided to take the big leap into home ownership. At the time I was a social studies and English teacher at Arthur Eddy Junior High School in Saginaw, Michigan. My salary, like all teaching salaries in the Midwest during the early 1960s, was very small—a bit less than $4,000 annually. Consequently there was little money for a down payment and therefore only a limited housing market was available to me.

Saginaw was a city of about 125,000 inhabitants at the time. Historically it had developed the way many other cities did—in concentric circles. The core area in the center of the city comprised the downtown shopping and services area. Around that core was a section with older homes, many of which had been divided into apartments. The area surrounding that belt contained several General Motors automobile plants and other manufacturing. The next circle was made up of the more recently built homes. The outermost ring included the outlying suburbs. The Saginaw River flowed through the center of the downtown area and effectively divided the city into two approximately equal halves. The upscale section of the city, with larger and more expensive homes, was found west of the river and conversely, the East Side was made up of smaller, less expensive homes.

My pocketbook rather than my architectural sensibilities determined where I should look to buy a house. Naturally, my heart's true desire was to have a home on the West Side. Ever since moving to Saginaw, and even long before that, I often drove through that area to admire the seemingly infinite variety of beautiful contemporary, colonial and ranch style homes it offered. I fairly salivated over the real estate opportunities one could find there. Alas, in home buying as in most other endeavors, one must begin small and work up the economic scale. Reluctantly I put away my "pie in the sky" architectural ideas and turned to more practical house hunting on the East Side.

After the real estate salesman had shown me several available homes in the less expensive section of town, I began to take heart and became more excited about buying there. What changed my attitude so quickly? The answer was very simple. All of the houses I toured were what would now be termed "fixer uppers." They were, in fact, the exact sort of house that I really desired, because I could turn loose my remodeling instincts and let my renovating desires soar. That is, of course, they could soar as high as my limited funds would allow. From that point on, in my house search, I concentrated on what each house could become if some time and money were spent on it; not on what it was at the moment. A number of the possibilities began to capture my imagination.

Eventually, after careful deliberation, I settled upon a small house on Whittier Street in a far East Side location. The house sat on the southwest corner where Whittier and Twentieth Streets crossed. The building lot was large and shaded by a pear tree, a crabapple tree and four stately old American elms. Those trees, especially the elms, influenced me greatly toward buying the house.

The house was solidly built of cinderblocks and was about ten years old at the time. It was painted a pale green with white trim and its roof was topped with black asphalt shingles. A colonial type lamppost stood at the outer end of the cement driveway. Whittier Street ended a little way past the house and since it was a cul-de-sac with only two houses—the one directly across the street and mine—there was little traffic.

The small ranch style house, with just under seven hundred square feet, was built on a cement slab. It contained a living room, kitchen, dining area, two bedrooms, a bathroom and a screened-in porch. (See the floor plans at the end of this chapter.) Besides the beautifully treed lot, there were several things that impressed me about the house itself.

First, it had cathedral ceilings in all the rooms, giving each a contemporary feeling of spaciousness. Also the windows in the living room and dining area were particularly large, extending from floor to ceiling, thus they flooded those rooms with lots of sunlight. In spite of the absence of a basement, there was plenty of storage space. The two bedrooms as well as the living room had fairly good sized closets and the screened-in porch boasted a fourteen foot wall of cupboards with shelves In addition there was a small linen closet in the hallway near the bathroom and the kitchen, too, had lots of storage.

Even more impressive than anything else about the house was its price and terms of sale. The total cost was only seven thousand dollars and the owner, a real estate company, was willing to sell it to me on a land contract with two hundred dollars down, an interest rate of six percent and monthly payments of only seventy-five dollars! That was somewhat less than the rent I had been paying on my apartment. I was ecstatic. It meant that I would have a little money left to do some of the renovating projects which already were whirling about in my super active imagination. Hot dog! I could hardly wait to put my name on the dotted line and begin my new adventure!

The ink was hardly dry on the land contract for the new house when I took on its first remodeling project. As you can see by the "before" floor plan at the end of this chapter, the original living room was rather small—only 12 ½ by 13 ½ feet. Keeping the house in the original footprint was extremely important to me because I lacked the money for an addition at the time. However, I thought of a way that the room could be enlarged without changing the overall size of the house. I would incorporate the dining area and a small part of the kitchen into the living room, thus making its size a very respectable 12 ½ by 20 ½ feet. (See the "after" floor plan at the end of this chapter.) The kitchen would still be large enough to be an "eat in" type even though a few square feet had been taken from it. For larger dinner parties I could set a table at the end of the new living room near the kitchen.

The renovation job was going to be messy because invariably all demolition and wall building projects are. Therefore, I did the main part of the remodeling even before moving from my apartment to the house. First, I removed the short divider wall between the living room and the dining area. Then I used 2' X 4' lumber to frame in the new wall between the living room and the kitchen and covered it with sheets of drywall. I taped and plastered the drywall joints and then sanded them smooth after the plaster had dried. Though the ceilings in both rooms (the kitchen and the living room) were cathedral type, I constructed the new wall only eight feet in height. My reasoning was that the entire house was heated with a wall furnace and the triangular space at the top of the wall would aid air circulation plus the shorter wall formed an attractive plant shelf.

Next I tackled the floors. Previously the living room had been carpeted and the dining area was covered with squares of vinyl tile. I used plaster to smooth the floor area where the former wall had been and then tore out the living room carpeting. Next I had the entire area, including the new living room and the bedroom hallway re-covered with wall-to-wall carpeting. After it was painted and the carpeting was in, the living room appeared as if it had always been that larger size.

So the first remodeling project on my new house came to a successful close. I was thrilled and proud of the result and immediately began moving into my own little "mansion." Buying a house and doing its first renovation have to be counted as important milestones in my life and they occurred in June of 1961 just a little over forty-seven years before I am now writing this chapter.

About a year later I learned that possession of a home may bring unhappiness as well as joy to the property owner. The culprit in that case was an ugly and almost microscopic little bug called the American bark beetle. Do you recall that I said there were four stately American elm trees on the property when I bought it?

Early in the summer of 1962 I noticed that some of the higher leaves on the elm trees were withering and turning yellow. In a few weeks that same problem had spread lower until most of the leaves were dead and the poor trees looked very sick indeed. The yellow leaves gave one the impression that we were having an especially early fall that year. Previously, when I noticed the first withered leaves, I called an arborist who told me that they probably had what is called Dutch elm disease. He said that it was caused by a fungus carried by the American bark beetle and he felt certain that the trees were doomed. The malady was called

Dutch elm disease because the fungus was discovered in the Netherlands, where it was spread by the European bark beetle, and it mainly infected elm trees. Eventually it crossed the Atlantic to New York City and then moved westward. At that time the disease was rapidly spreading across Michigan and would likely be the end of all the American elms in the state. I was devastated because those trees were important in my decision to buy the house. By the end of the summer my beautiful and stately elms were stark, dead skeletons.

With the help of a couple of friends and a chain saw, I cut the skeletons down and burned them. The arborist had told me it was the only way to destroy the fungus so we had huge bonfires going for days on end. We had purposely sawn the trees off near to the ground but still the yard looked like a cemetery with the trunks serving as grave markers. I felt the loss greatly, but was eager to clean up the mess so I hired a neighbor who had a machine that ground the trunks into sawdust. That we took in large bags to the land fill facility.

Only partially daunted by my landscaping tragedy, I went to the nursery and bought four small Chinese elms, a purple leaf fig tree and a clump of white bark birch and transplanted them as replacements for the lost trees. I had read that the Chinese elms are unaffected by the Dutch elm disease fungus, so felt safe in using them. All but one of the trees wintered well but of course, the one that failed was the most expensive. The Chinese elms cost under ten dollars each, the fig cost about twelve dollars but, the birch cost over thirty-two dollars. The following spring that little birch tree girded its loins and gave its best shot, but only managed to produce three little leaves before expiring in a blaze of ignominy. Over ten dollars per leaf was definitely not an approved part of my budgetary plans for replacing the trees in the yard, so I mourned loss of the birch.

I lived in the Whittier Street house for another five years after that dreadful summer and during that time the Chinese elms and the purple leaf plum flourished. When I put the house up for sale in 1967 the elms had grown to a height of about twenty feet and once more the lot was starting to look a little like the lovely one that I had purchased in 1961. The Chinese elm trees did not have the long, graceful arching limbs that the American elms had, but they did serve as suitable, though less beautiful, substitutes for the originals. The plum tree was a very welcome addition to the lot because it gave some relief from the otherwise totally green palette and added variety to the landscape.

My remodeling activities in the house during that time were concentrated mainly in the bathroom. I put ceramic tile in the tub enclosure and replaced the shower curtain with sliding glass doors, covered the vinyl floor tile with turquoise carpeting matching that in the living room, replaced the wall-hung sink with a decorative wood vanity and added a glass-fronted towel storage unit. When all that was finished, it still was a very small bathroom, but it definitely was a well appointed and attractive small bathroom.

On an extremely cold day one winter the wall furnace breathed its last and expired while I was at school teaching. My first clue that something was amiss was when I came home and saw water running down the driveway and freezing there. Not only was the house cold but an added problem was that some of the more exposed plumbing pipes in the kitchen had frozen and burst. Water found its way under the kitchen door, into the screened porch and then down the driveway. Plumbing was one of the building skills which I had only attempted, but never successfully, so I called in the experts to replace the furnace and the burst pipes. As I watched the plumbers at their intricate and complicated work, it only reinforced my belief that I had made a wise decision in hiring them.

My first few years on Whittier Street proved to me that being a home owner had downs as well as ups. But when I examined the pros and cons of both renting and owning, the latter always came out on the heavier end of the scale. Now, nearly fifty years later, I am still of the exact same opinion and would far prefer being an owner over being a renter. Apparently some people are just slow learners.

THE WHITTIER STREET HOUSE

SAGINAW, MICHIGAN - JUNE, 1961

MY LITTLE MANSION
(FRONT & EAST SIDE)

BACK & EAST SIDE
(NOTICE THE NEIGHBOR'S DRIVE)

FRONT & WEST SIDE
(PLUS MY FORD FALCON)

THE NEW HOMEOWNER
(IN THE REMODELED LIVING ROOM)

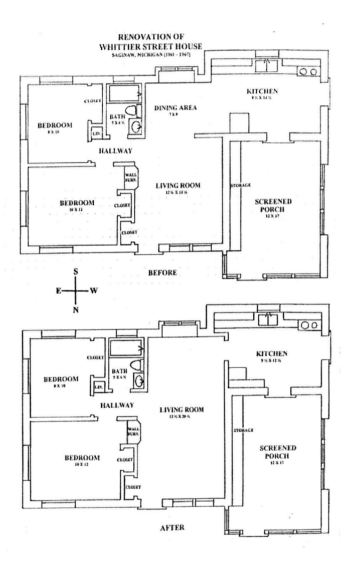

Chapter Five

Moving Up

A true, dyed in the wool, remodeler or renovator is never really satisfied with the place where he is living at any given time. He is always looking to better his residential situation in some manner. That aphorism has fit me like a glove all of my life. I have lived in a large number of places and during the time I was in each of them I was constantly casting about for ways to either make improvements in my living situation or, if the opportunity presented itself, then moving on to yet another one. Dissatisfaction seemed to be a way of life for me.

I thoroughly enjoyed buying my first house and spending the next six years making improvements in it, as described in the previous chapter. When I had done nearly all that was possible to that house, considering its location in the downscale East Side section of Saginaw, I began to look further afield. Naturally my attention turned to the more up-scale area of the city, the West Side. I had coveted living in that part of the city since moving to Saginaw and felt that it was the right time to make the move. So, once again I went house hunting.

Before I toured the first available house with the realtor, I made a list of the qualities I was looking for in a new residence. I wanted a West Side location, mature trees on the property, a contemporary style, a cathedral ceiling in the living room, a fireplace, a second living area such as a family room, three bedrooms, at least one and a half bathrooms, an attached garage and a price that was within my budget. To me that list seemed very reasonable, but my real estate representative saw it in a much different light. The sticking point ended up being the last item on the list—the price. There were many homes available with all the other qualities I had listed, but very few in the price range I was able to afford. That reprehensible ogre called "economics" once more was rearing its ugly head in the same way it had when I sought my first house.

I daresay that the realtor and I inspected between thirty and forty houses with little or no success. All of them were either totally without charm, lacking in one or more of the items on my want list, or were priced out of my range. We both began to despair of every finding a house that could satisfy me. Often I would drive up and down the streets on the West Side searching for realtor's signs. When I found one, I would size the house up to see if it were even close to what I was looking for. Usually it fell far short of the mark, but once in a while I was lucky, and it seemed to fit my needs. Then I would have my realtor make an appointment for a walk-through of the house. After a closer look I usually was doomed to disappointment. That dogged and obviously painful process went on for several months. Normally I love to go through houses—it is one of my favorite avocations—but after having seen a virtual multitude of unsuitable examples, that too began to lose its charm for me.

The house search began in the late spring, continued all through the summer and on into the fall before my luck changed. One brisk but sunny day, when the leaves were turning to their fall colors, the realtor called me with exciting news. He had located a house that he thought fit all my criteria. He gave me the address on Brockway Street and asked if I would drive by it before he made an appointment to see it. Obviously he had become rather chary of wasting his time on appointments that came to nothing. I did the drive-by and during that cursory inspection, noted nothing negative other than the house was rather uninspired in its exterior decoration. The poor thing definitely lacked curb appeal but since that was something I could provide; it did not deter me at all.

All of the following came about in rapid succession. I called the realtor, he made an appointment and we toured the house. I knew immediately it was the perfect place for me as, surprisingly, it met all of my criteria. After signing the purchase agreement, I paid the earnest money to the real estate company and was amazed when my first offer was accepted by the owner. I knew I was well on the way toward owning the home. Only at that time did the realization hit me that if the purchase were to go through, I would then be the owner of two houses, not one. I certainly lacked the economic wherewithal to be that financially burdened so I listed my East Side house immediately.

In today's housing market when someone sets out to buy a home, usually he goes to the lending institution first and is "pre-approved" in advance for a certain amount of loan. In the 1960s that was not the practice. Instead the prospective buyer located the house he wished to buy and only then approached the bank for a loan. That often made for some nervous, nail-biting waiting periods between the application time and the date on which the sale actually took place. Sometimes it caused the house buying experience to fall apart completely. Naturally the prospective owner is excited and views the upcoming sale with eager anticipation, but if the loan were disapproved by the lending institution, then that hope would be dashed to the ground, or at least delayed while other arrangements were made.

Two vexing issues presented themselves in my negotiations to purchase the Brockway Street house. The first of those problems was that my initial loan application was turned down by the bank. It was disapproved because my yearly teaching salary was slightly below the amount necessary to carry that size of loan. No problem. I was able to overcome that obstacle by presenting the bank officials with proof that I recently had invested in a partnership in a local restaurant. From that investment I earned a small salary which easily put my annual income over the top. With that added information, the bank officials approved the loan application.

The second issue that gave me pause was that my other house on Whittier Street did not sell immediately. A young couple was very interested in it but they seemed unable to come up with the necessary loan. While they were seeking other avenues for financing the deal, their real estate agent suggested that they temporarily rent my house and later, when their loan was approved, the house sale would be consummated. Reluctantly I agreed to that plan of action because, though it was not ideal, it made the best of a bad situation. Fortunately before the agreement went into effect, however, the couple was approved for the necessary financing and thus could buy the house immediately. That was an enormous load off my mind.

I was very excited about finally reaching my goal of moving to the West Side of Saginaw. Especially thrilling to me was the fact that though the house was far from ideal, it did have most of what I wanted in a residence. Those included a cathedral ceiling and a beautiful stone fireplace in the living room, a separate family room, three bedrooms, a full bathroom plus a half bath and it boasted a car and a half attached garage. The 1,300 square foot house was well situated on a nicely landscaped lot with large trees. In my estimation the residence was a perfect fit for me because it did have some faults. That meant I would have the fun of doing renovations while I lived there.

As mentioned already the home lacked curb appeal so that was a problem I tackled early on. One obvious exterior fault was that there were two front doors. One of the two was the original main entrance just to the right of a central cathedral style window. I kept that one where it was. The other door, also on the front elevation, was further toward the right side of the house. The room into which it led had been converted from a carport to a family room and had louvered windows on its south and east sides. That style of window made the space into what is usually called a Florida room. I removed that door, paneled the blank space and painted it the same as the rest of the house. It blended perfectly and there no longer was any confusion as to where the front door was located. (See the "before" photo at the end of this chapter. The extra front door had already been removed by the time that picture was taken.)

Like my first house, on Whittier Street, this one, too, was built of cinder blocks. But the difference lay in the fact that the builder had added a fascia of bricks to the outside walls. In the center of the house's front side was a tall triple window extending to the pointed roof peak. At the base of that window was a large planter of grey cut stone which matched the stone on the fireplace chimney as well as that on several other planters along the front and sides of the house. The home had a gravel covered built-up type of roof and the entire place was painted a very pale green. The problem was that there was no contrast. Everything had either the same color—gray—or a pale green of the same intensity.

My solution was to paint the walls a creamy white and then provide contrast by painting the outer edges of the wide overhanging eaves plus the door and window trim all a rich chocolate brown. This resulted in a differentiation in both color and intensity between the gray cut stone, the dark brown trim and the creamy white walls. (See the before and after photos at the end of this chapter.)

The interior of the Brockway house needed serious remodeling mainly in the kitchen. Between the dining end of the living room and the kitchen was a breakfast bar. I thought it was ugly and soon tore it out. In its place I put a floor to ceiling bookcase on the living room side and a shallow storage cabinet on the kitchen side. Those two additions effectively kept guests in the living room from getting a clear view of the food preparation area.

Though the kitchen was rather small—about ten by twelve feet, it had a hookup for a washer and dryer. Because I regularly sent all of my laundry out to be washed and ironed, I knew full well that I wouldn't be using those appliances while I lived there. So I decided to replace them with a built in upholstered banquette which formed a small eating area to substitute for the breakfast bar I had removed earlier. (The washer and dryer hook-up remained hidden behind the back of the banquette.)

The main bathroom also received some fairly serious attention from me. I got rid of the plastic tile and put ceramic tile in the shower surround, replaced the shower curtain with glass doors, added a new medicine cabinet and put modern lighting over the sink. After the walls were papered in a contemporary design, the room fairly sparkled.

The balance of the house required little other than redecorating. The walls in the living room and two of the three bedrooms were a dismal gold color and patterned draperies further darkened those rooms. In contrast the third bedroom, which I used as a study, had draperies which blended nicely with the paneling there so I kept its décor as I found it. I painted the walls and put up new draperies in the living room, the family room, the kitchen and the two bedrooms.

When all the changes had been made, my favorite room in the house turned out to be the elegant living room. It was about eleven by twenty-two feet in size capped by a beautiful redwood cathedral ceiling. Opposite the tall window on the front was a gray natural stone fireplace wall which rose to the peak. After the other three walls were painted an off white and white draperies were hung at the windows, the room was extremely bright and cheerful. To furnish it I chose overstuffed pieces in earth tones of brown, tan and rust with a few orange and blue accents for contrast. During the seven years I lived in the Brockway house that room also became a popular gathering place for friends as well as my extended family. We enjoyed many holiday get-togethers there with a cheerful fire in the hearth.

THE BROCKWAY HOUSE REMODEL
Saginaw, Michigan - 1967

BEFORE

AFTER

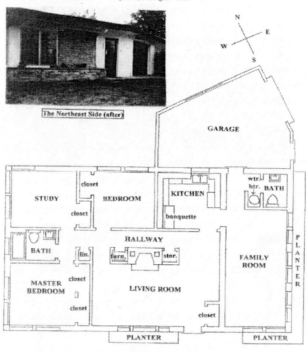

THE BROCKWAY HOUSE REMODEL
Saginaw, Michigan - 1967

The Northeast Side (after)

Chapter Six

An A-Frame on the Water

As I grow older I have become more and more aware that my thinking about architectural style has gone through a real metamorphosis over the years. My earliest memory of actually having a preference in building style is from about the age of twelve or thirteen. I was in junior high and early high school at the time and thought that the salt-box style was the most pleasing to the eye. From that early beginning my preference turned for a time to the popular ranch style house and then later I developed a strong liking for the Cape Cod style. During my early twenties, my architectural interests took a distinctly different turn. I was in college at the time and because of the strong impact of several of my art instructors, became enamored of Frank Lloyd Wright's architecture. His influence can be seen in the first house that I purchased in Saginaw. Two of the things that drew me to it were its floor-to-ceiling windows and its cathedral ceilings—both were usual characteristics of Wright's designs. Also, a couple of the important criteria I desired in my second house were that it must be of the style then called "contemporary" and that it also must include cathedral ceilings.

Though Frank Lloyd Wright did not invent the A-Frame, the houses he designed late in his career, with soaring ceilings, certainly were forerunners or harbingers of that type of house and I thought them particularly attractive. Therefore it is only natural and logical that I give Wright much of the credit for influencing me toward the A-Frame as my eventual preferred house style. That preference probably lasted for least a couple of decades.

Early in the fall of 1970 I had my first chance to own and renovate a home with A-Frame styling. At the time I was sharing my Brockway Street residence in Saginaw with a housemate, named Steve. Late that summer, the two of us were invited for a weekend visit with a couple who had a cottage at Lake James. Lake James is a small, man-made body of water located just east of Prudenville, Michigan, about eighty miles northwest of Saginaw. The lake was roughly ten years old at the time and it had been formed when a developer did some excavation in a woodsy area near there and then built an earthen dam across Denton Creek. The end result was a relatively small and shallow body of water approximately two miles from east to west and likely about three quarters of a mile at its widest from north to south.

During our weekend visit, Steve and I noticed that there was an empty cottage next door to the one owned by our hosts. What a derelict it was! The structure was likely one of the ugliest A-Frames in existence at the time. It had vertical siding which was painted barn red and was trimmed in white, however most of its surfaces were badly weathered. The pie-shaped lot, narrower at the lake front, was a tangle of wild brush, trees and weeds. Its condition indicated clearly that no care had been expended on it since the cottage was built. On the first floor at the lake side there was a small window on either side of a center door. Because of that unfortunate arrangement one could see very little of the lake from the interior of the cottage. What a shame that such a picturesque view was being ignored.

The A-Frame itself was a mere shell as none of the interior rooms had been finished off. The only heat was provided by two clearly inadequate electric baseboard heaters. That meant the un-insulated cottage could only be occupied during the warmer months of the year. The building was electrified, but the wiring was a jumble of seemingly disconnected cables with little organization or electrical planning. One could see from one end of the cottage through to the other because most of the walls and ceilings were merely framed in and very little drywall had been applied to them thus far. The only bathroom was a two-piece lavatory equipped with a sink and stool, but no tub or shower. There was an electrical pump to draw water from the well, plus a hot water heater but they, too, were surrounded only by a framework with no solid walls. The floor was a cement slab and had a long crack along its center. A rough stairway with no handrails led to the second floor. There about half of the area was without flooring, thus one could see through the floor joists to the lower floor.

All in all the mistreated A-Frame appeared to be an orphan badly in need of adoption, and, as such, both Steve and I found it extremely intriguing. We talked excitedly all weekend about what a fascinating project it would be to purchase the cottage jointly and then use our sweat-equity and ingenuity to bring it up to its full potential. The cottage presented a most tantalizing prospect.

Our weekend hosts informed us that the cottage was owned by a couple who had lived in Flint, Michigan. A job transfer caused their moving to Littletown, Ohio; consequently they had scant time to spend at a secondary residence and only visited it a few times each year. Unfortunately the A-Frame was thus abandoned to the forces of nature during the balance of the time. Steve and I learned the names and telephone number of the owners and called them that very weekend. We were thrilled to learn that they *were* willing to sell the cottage. Immediately we wrote a purchase agreement and sent it to them. Within a couple of weeks they accepted our terms and about a month later we held the official closing. Therefore in early October we became the proud owners of the heretofore neglected A-Frame.

I would like to digress long enough to relate an interesting tale about our buying the property. When we sent the purchase agreement to the cottage owners, I made a vow to myself. If they accept our terms for the purchase I will quit smoking immediately. The couple did accept the agreement so I put away my cigarettes, but told no one. I thought that it was interesting and comical that more than a week went by before any of my friends, including Steve, noticed that I no longer was puffing tobacco smoke into my lungs. Today, a little over thirty-eight years later, I still don't.

Because Michigan's frigid winter was nearly upon us we had to act quickly. We purchased a wall furnace which was fueled by bottled gas and had it installed the next weekend. I recall that the heater, which was obviously too small for the square footage of the un-insulated space, ran nonstop from the time we arrived each weekend on Friday evening until we left on Sunday afternoon to return home. It did, however, provide heat enough for us to work on the renovation for the unexpectedly short time we had left that particular winter.

By working feverishly each weekend Steve and I made many improvements on the interior of the cottage. Unfortunately all of that fine progress came to an abrupt end around the middle of December. The weekend was very cold and as usual we arrived at the cottage after dark on Friday evening. We turned on the lights and then checked to see that the water system was working properly. We soon learned that the pump ran fine but no water emerged from the faucets. After looking more closely we determined that the underground water pipe leading from the outside well to the water pump must be frozen. That is something which happens often during winters in the Midwest so Michigan people are accustomed to it. Generally they thaw the frozen water pipes by heating them with a blow torch but, because the well's supply pipe was made of plastic, no heat could be applied to it. What should we do?

We were in a quandary. How could we spend weekends at the cottage with no water? Of course that also meant that the toilet would not flush. After a hurried conference, we decided to put our remodeling plans on hold for the balance of the winter and wait until the natural warmth from the upcoming spring thawed the plastic pipe and allowed us to have running water again. We cancelled our weekend renovation plans and, disappointed, drove back to Saginaw later that evening.

For the rest of that winter we would occasionally drive to the A-Frame, but only to check on things, consequently it remained in its incomplete state. Our frustration knew no bounds because we both were excited about the progress made already and, of course, wished to continue with it. Finally, in March the supply pipe thawed and the water flowed freely when we turned on the pump. Once more we were able to go back to our intriguing project.

Eagerly the two of us started in again and that first year we accomplished a great deal. If my memory serves me correctly, we insulated the walls and ceilings, in addition to altering the windows and doors on the lake side to improve the view from the interior. We changed the stairway's location and removed the ceiling joists from the rear third of the structure. What remained of the second floor then became a large bedroom loft overlooking the lower level. We constructed a two-foot-wide bridge from the loft to a narrow balcony at the back where new sliding doors allowed a view of the lake from the upper floor as well. In addition those doors gave us access to an exterior balcony at the back of the A-Frame.

We paneled the walls throughout the cottage and divided the lower level of the lake side into a living room with a dining area and kitchen along its west side. Next to the kitchen we enclosed a combination pantry and utility room to house the water pump, the water heater and some shelving for groceries and miscellaneous items. Toward the street side of the A-Frame we divided the space into a small bedroom, an entrance hallway and a bathroom. In addition, we re-wired and re-plumbed most of the cottage. With the exception of the utility room and bathroom, we carpeted the entire upper and lower levels.

Steve and I worked with equal diligence on the exterior of the A-Frame. We cut back the brush throughout the lot, planted grass seed, trimmed the trees and put in a few small evergreens and flowerbeds here and there on the property. Along the roadside we built a simple ornamental fence. We painted the exterior of the cottage a cream color with chocolate brown trim. For contrast we did the front and back doors in a rich gold color and then added black shutters at the sides of the front door as well as the window above it. On the lake side, we added a hand rail to the exterior upstairs balcony. (See the "before" and "after" photos at the end of this chapter.)

We improved the sandy driveway by hauling in gravel and then used paving blocks to build a sidewalk from it to the front door. Down at the beach front we completely rebuilt the decrepit dock and tore out the lake weeds by hand to make an improved swimming area. That was very helpful because it wasn't until a couple of years later that we put a shower in the bathroom. Therefore we often took baths in the lake. From the time we first owned the A-Frame, the well water was somewhat brackish, apparently because it was from a very shallow well. To solve that problem we had a deeper well drilled. Later we also purchased the lot next door toward the east, put up a snowmobile shed and then a year later added a workshop to its far side.

Steve and I enjoyed the A-Frame as a cottage for several years. During most of that time I lived there for my summer vacations from teaching and Steve would join me on the weekends. Both of us found Lake James a wonderful place to spend our time and we relished its forested, lakeside ambiance. I bought a motor boat for water skiing, Steve bought a sailboat and we each had snowmobiles for the winter. We met a number of the other cottage owners and began to develop a social circle there. Eventually Lake James began to seem more like home than Saginaw did.

Prudenville, a half mile west of Lake James, joins the village of Houghton Lake and Houghton Lake Heights to cover the south and west shores of the lake. Houghton

Lake is the largest inland body of water in Michigan. The permanent year-round population of the area is probably about 10,000 in total but weekend tourists increase the number to about 100,000. Steve and I thought that the Prudenville area was wonderful but not everyone agreed with us. I recall attending a rather posh party in suburban Detroit and someone asking me where I lived. When I replied, "Prudenville." His snooty response was, "On purpose?" Occasionally, when asked that question I would use an exaggerated French pronunciation of the name—Pru – dawn – VEEL—in my best French accent. That usually stumped most people. They had no idea where I lived but generally lacked the nerve to ask me a second time.

For several years Steve had been making decorative metal sculptures which he sold at art shows and at various locations in Prudenville as well as the Saginaw and Bay City area. He had gained success as an artist, and early in 1975 made the decision to leave his office manager's position in Saginaw and become a full-time metal sculptor. Steve was starting out relatively small and consequently could not be certain of a steady income. We discussed the situation and made the decision that both of us could save money by moving permanently to the cottage. That, of course meant that we would no longer be supporting two residences—one in Saginaw and the other in Prudenville. The plan meant that during the school year I would be driving back and forth daily from the A-Frame to my teaching job in Midland—nearly sixty miles each way. Gasoline prices were much lower than presently, so at the time it seemed like a practical plan.

Steve needed a larger workshop for his metal sculpting business, so prior to the move; we remodeled the combination snowmobile shed and workshop to serve in that capacity. We put a large opening between the two areas making the 12 X 16 foot space into one room, plus added windows, ventilation and a small furnace. That summer, after the move, we also built a chalet-style double garage for housing the cars and the snowmobiles. The garage's large second floor also provided badly needed storage.

The metal sculpture venture was very successful for Steve. In fact he still practices it today at that same location, over thirty years later. A couple of years after our move to Prudenville, we added on to the cottage by building a living room on its east side. The new 12'x18' room boasted a fireplace on the front and a wide picture window on the lake side. A large opening gave access to the older part of the house. That additional square footage made the house too large for the furnace we previously had installed; therefore we replaced it with an entire new heating system with flues to all the rooms.

In a very few years the 120 mile round trip commute to Midland began to pall. I left home at 6:00 each morning in order to get to school on time and frequently at that hour the snowplows hadn't yet cleared the roads. In addition, early one morning I hit a large male deer on the highway just south of Prudenville while en route. The collision did several thousand dollars worth of damage to the vehicle and it couldn't be driven from the scene of the accident. Also, the badly injured deer unfortunately had to be killed. The buck had attempted to jump over the hood of the car, but misjudged and didn't make it. Instead it landed on the hood and broke both back legs. The luckless animal managed to drag itself into the woods at the side of the road where the investigating officer found it and put it out of its misery.

That grisly incident shook me up badly and from then on I was extremely tense during the hour-long drive. There were literally thousands of deer in the forested area between Prudenville and Midland and usually I would see more than twenty during each trip. Subsequently, for a few months I rented a room near my school and only went home on weekends, but that was far from a satisfactory solution to the problem.

Eventually, in 1979, I came to the difficult and sad conclusion that I should leave the lakeside A-Frame. I decided to move to an apartment in Midland while I looked for a house to purchase there. Fortunately for me, Steve was willing to buy my half interest in the Lake James property so we agreed on a price and concluded the deal. As an interesting side note, Steve still lives there today. Since that time he has added on to the A-frame in every direction but *down*. It is hardly recognizable as the same building we first saw during the summer of 1970. The once neglected little cottage has blossomed into a large and luxurious home.

REMODELING THE A-FRAME
Prudenville, Michigan (1970 – 1979)

VIEW OF THE LAKE FRONT

ROAD SIDE - BEFORE

ROAD SIDE - AFTER

LAKE SIDE - BEFORE

LAKE SIDE - AFTER

REMODELING THE A-FRAME
Prudenville, Michigan (1970 – 1979)

ROAD SIDE
(AFTER GARAGE WAS BUILT)

ROAD SIDE
(AFTER LIVING ROOM WAS BUILT)

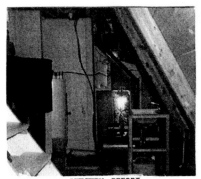

KITCHEN - BEFORE

KITCHEN - AFTER

Chapter Seven

I *Really* Want a Swimming Pool!

Near the end of the 1970s I purchased my first house in Midland, where I had been teaching for about twelve years. When I left the Saginaw school position for the one in Midland, I was already firmly entrenched in my house on the West Side of the city and was averse to leaving it. I loved the house and its location, but especially satisfying to me was that I had attained my goal of moving from the downscale East Side to the upscale and coveted West Side. In addition, Midland's Central Intermediate School and my Saginaw home were only about eighteen miles apart. Consequently I elected to remain where I was, for the time being anyway. The daily roundtrip of less than forty miles presented little or no burden.

Over the next decade or so, my living situation changed as you probably already noted from reading the previous chapter titled, "An A-Frame on the Water". Suffice it to say that after several moves, the fall of 1979 found me living in a one-bedroom garden level apartment on Bayliss Street in Midland. Though I have lived in several apartments during my adult years, paying rent for and renovating other people's spaces no longer appealed to me as much as it once had. From the start I thought of that small dwelling as merely a stop-gap measure. I fully planned to buy a house as soon as I found one that suited my tastes and pocketbook.

The three room apartment, though only a temporary residence, did have one really important aspect in its favor. The cement patio off my living room backed up to the apartment complex's swimming pool and I came to enjoy that feature very much during the relatively short time I lived there. Probably by that time mental seeds already were being planted in my brain that it would be really nice to have a pool included with my next house. Reinforcing that idea was the fact that prior to moving I had lived for several years at Prudenville where I had Lake James at my back door and could take daily swims whenever the weather permitted.

I spent much of that fall looking at and touring houses that were for sale and at first only concentrated on those with swimming pools. The real estate saleswoman tried her best to fulfill my desire for that particular luxury, but it simply did not work out. Each house that she showed me, with a pool included, was invariably priced far out of my range and conversely, those within my range were without pools. Once again, my economic situation was at odds with my idealistic cravings. As was usually the case, economics won out and so I was forced to settle for a house without a swimming pool. Though it was defeated for the moment, the desire for a pool did not die completely; instead it peacefully retreated and became temporarily dormant in my brain, merely waiting for the opportune time to re-emerge.

After viewing a large number of houses, the one I chose to buy was a small ranch style home at the end of a short cul-de-sac called East Campbell Court. The thousand square foot house was quite different from most of my previous abodes. It was a single story dwelling with a living room, kitchen, three bedrooms, one bathroom, and a moderately sized screened porch. One of the smaller bedrooms at the back of the house was situated so it could serve as a dining room and that was how I used it while living there. The house had a full, unfinished basement. At the end of the cement driveway was a detached one and a half car garage. The frame home was clad with oversized cedar shingles that had been painted a harvest gold color and the trim work was painted a mousy gray-brown. Obviously those were not even close to my idea of good color choices for the house.

Before moving in I already had plans in my head for making several changes. The first of those involved the existing heating system. In the basement was an antiquated oil furnace with an enormous storage tank next to it. The entire house constantly smelled of scorched oil. It was worse, of course, during the heating season, but still detectable all year long. The very day that I closed on the house, I hired a heating man to replace the furnace with a new, gas forced-air furnace. When that was done I advertised for someone willing to remove the oil storage tank if I gave him its contents. A man showed up the next day and the tank was gone within a week. Already I had made good progress..

Next I turned to the unattached garage. The structure was sixteen feet wide and twenty feet long. There was an off-center, single eight foot overhead door on the front. That small entrance, of course, allowed only one car to be stored there. I was planning to have a tenant living in the residence with me and wanted both of us to be able to keep our autos in the garage. That problem was solved when I enlisted the help of my brother-in-law, Richard, who was very handy with carpentry tools.

In only two days we had the building remodeled. After removing the garage door and enlarging the front opening, we put in a new fourteen foot wide overhead door. We moved the old single garage door to the rear of the building so that I would have access through the garage to that part of the back yard. I planned to store my small outboard speed boat there. Fortunately, both my new housemate and I owned compact type cars and, though there was little room to spare, the two vehicles fit easily into the new garage. (See the "before" and "after" plans and photos at the end of this chapter.)

The harvest gold exterior with the mousey gray-brown trim was the next thing to go. I painted both the house and garage a deep, chocolate brown and trimmed them in white. To accent those colors I painted the window shutters, the front door and the new garage door a rich creamy beige color. What a difference those changes made.

Almost overnight, instead of being ashamed of it, I was thrilled to turn onto my street and see the little jewel of a house proudly dominating the east end of our cul-de-sac.

When I had lived in the little house on East Campbell Court for a little over a year, the swimming pool bug bit me again, though much harder that time. It seemed as though I was constantly reminded of how pleasant the pool at the Bayliss Street apartment had been and what fun I had swimming in the lake at Prudenville when I lived there. Every home magazine I picked up that year seemed to feature people enjoying pools of all sizes and configurations. My besotted imagination told me that there must be some way that I too could afford to become a member of the "POOLED" class of home owners.

About five or six years prior to that time I made a trip to New York State to visit my younger brother and his family. Dan, his wife, Judy, and their four children, lived in a handsome old Italianate style house in historic Sodus, a small town roughly thirty miles east of Rochester and near the Lake Ontario shore. When the family first moved there, a few years previously, they had rented half of that same house which was divided at the time. Since then they had bought the house and had spread into the entire residence. The children were in their early teens or younger and loved the water, so Dan had put an above-ground pool in the back yard. It had a high fence around it and a small raised deck along one side. I recalled that all of us, adults and children alike, had a wonderful weekend playing in the pool.

I loved the thought that I could have the luxury of swimming right in my backyard, and an above-ground pool was well within my financial means, but I intensely disliked one very important thing about them. That was their appearance. I think that all above-ground swimming pools are unsightly at best. My brother's was no exception to that rule of thumb. It was unattractive and, in my estimation, was an ugly blot on an otherwise attractive backyard. Having said that, however, I hasten to add that there is one extremely positive fact about those pools—they are inexpensive.

Though my economic situation had improved greatly over the years due to teacher unionization and regular salary increases, my income was still not one that could afford the high cost of the usual in-ground swimming pool. Most quotes I heard at that time ranged from about $15,000 on up to $25,000 depending on how many extras were included. I was far too practical to spend nearly an entire year's salary on a luxury which could be used only five months of the year and would sit idle for the balance.

Most people have their own individualized methods of solving problems. When I come up against a building or remodeling project that stumps me for a time, I generally attempt to find a solution through the use of drawings of various schemes the problem suggests to me. I am a very visual person and sometimes can become rather creative when presented with a pencil and a blank sheet of paper. That was the route I took to solve the swimming pool problem. First I wrote down the central issue at the top of the page. It was:

ALL ABOVE-GROUND POOLS ARE UNSIGHTLY. THEREFORE WHAT METHOD CAN I DEVISE WHICH WOULD REMOVE MY POOL FROM PUBLIC VIEW?

I spent hours upon hours and wasted enough paper to destroy a small forest before I found a solution which satisfied me. I purchased a round above-ground swimming pool twelve feet across and with five-foot sidewalls. My original plan was to excavate, by hand, a circular hole in the back yard three and one half feet deep and sixteen feet from side to side. When I had removed the sod and my shovel bit into the hard layer of soil just below, I quickly changed my mind. The clay was rock hard and therefore it gave me serious second thoughts. With those thoughts came visions of it taking all summer and fall to dig the excavation and then our not being able to use the pool until about Christmas time. Believe me when I say that Michigan winters are not conducive to outdoor swimming. Plan B involved my hiring a man and his small bulldozer to dig the hole for me.

The dozer operator made very short work of the excavation but there was one drawback. His efforts left me with a hole of the proper size but next to it was a huge pile of dirt taking up a large share of the rest of the backyard. It had not my intention to build a "Mount Davis" behind my house, but I had accomplished it anyway. Fortunately the front yard was a large one, so, as a temporary solution to the problem, I had the dozer operator move the pile there. An idea was slowly evolving in my brain about what the pile's possible future use might be. But I'm getting ahead of my story, so let's go back to the pool excavation in the rear yard.

I leveled the bottom of the hole and then assembled the pool in the center of it. When that was finished I had a two foot area all the way around the pool that later could be for access to maintain its exterior walls. To keep the sides of the excavation from eroding toward the pool, I covered them in sheets of scrap metal which were anchored in place. The scrap metal was from a discarded pool that I agreed to take off a friend's hands. He had no use for it and was happy to see the last of it.

Next I built a framework for a four-foot wide, many-sided deck that would go all around the pool and become part of a larger deck leading to the exterior wall of the screened porch. (See the "AFTER" deck and pool plan at the end of this chapter.) Later I covered the entire deck with treated 2' by 6's. The level of the new deck was the same height as the floor of the screened porch. That gave direct access from porch to the pool with no steps between. (See the drawings and photos at the end of this chapter.)

The net result of my project was that I had what appeared to be a circular in-ground pool surrounded by a multi-sided deck about a foot and a half higher than the lawn. The decking 2' by 6's abutted the top rail of the above ground pool so that it was not obvious unless one really looked for it. Landscaping around the new deck completed the project and further hid the above-ground pool from the casual observer.

You are likely wondering what happened to all the soil that the bulldozer excavated from the cavity and brought around to the front yard, aren't you? Small hills in lawns, called berms, were all the rage during the 1970s and 1980s so I decided that the dirt would be the raw material for my own berm. I smoothed the rough pile that the bulldozer had left into an undulating hill, about four feet high at the tallest and covering about a third of the front yard. On top of that I replanted the sod that I had removed from the new pool area and filled in the gaps with grass seed. In a short time my formerly flat, dull front yard was made more much more interesting with a grassy berm where none had previously existed. (See the "AFTER" photo at the end of this chapter.)

Over the next couple of years the berm became a popular play area for some of the neighborhood children, especially the boys. Apparently they played "King of the Mountain" and other games while I was at work and gone from the house during the day. I never actually saw them on the hill but often found their rubber balls and other toys there when I got home in the evening. So the swimming pool project had yet another serendipitous effect in the neighborhood; it provided entertainment for the youth of the area.

I relished using my combination "in-ground/above-ground" pool for several summers and hosted many parties there for friends, family and also for my colleagues at the school where I was teaching. The combination of screened porch, deck and pool, all connected, made it a great warm-weather party venue that could be enjoyed by everyone. Even my mother, who was in her late seventies and hadn't been swimming for decades, was persuaded to take a dip now and then. I particularly recall one memorable teachers' party where two of my colleagues imbibed just a bit more alcohol than they probably should have. They both took a late evening swim in the pool while fully clothed and found it not only pleasant, but sobering as well.

HOUSE ON EAST CAMPBELL CT.
MIDLAND, MICHIGAN
GARAGE, POOL & DECK

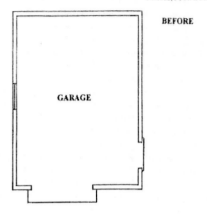

BEFORE

GARAGE

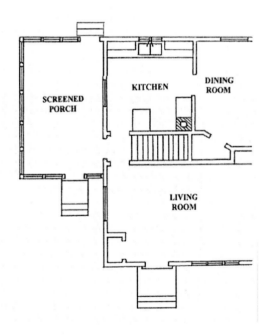

SCREENED PORCH

KITCHEN

DINING ROOM

LIVING ROOM

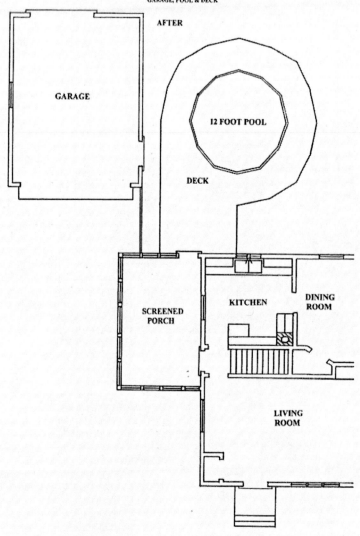

HOUSE ON EAST CAMPBELL CT.
MIDLAND, MICHIGAN
GARAGE, POOL & DECK

AFTER

GARAGE

12 FOOT POOL

DECK

SCREENED
PORCH

KITCHEN

DINING
ROOM

LIVING
ROOM

HOUSE ON EAST CAMPBELL
COURT
Midland, Michigan

New Pool and Deck
(Above ground pool placed in ground)

New Berm
(Soil was from the pool excavation)

Remodeled Garage
(A car & a half garage became a two
car garage)

Chapter Eight

A Debacle with a Happy Ending

I have bought and sold quite a number of houses during my renovating career and, as a result, have occasionally found myself in some unusual financial situations. The most bizarre of those occurred when I attempted to buy my second house in Midland, Michigan.

About five years after purchasing my first Midland home, on East Campbell Court, I was overcome with an urge to move on. During those few years in that house, I had put in a pool, erected a large deck, remodeled the garage, built a landscaping berm in the front yard, replaced the furnace and finished half of the basement into a family room, a bathroom and a bedroom. In addition, on the main floor I had remodeled the bathroom, built additional cupboards in the kitchen, renovated the screened porch and added a number of landscaping details here and there on the premises.

Thus, I had done every type of renovating on the house that I felt was prudent considering its location. Logic told me that if I were to sink any more money into it, there would be little chance of getting it back when the house was sold. Since a true-blue remodeler like me simply could not endure having no house to work on, I went shopping for one.

In a relatively short time I located the house that eventually was to become my next residence. It was on Sinclair Street, in a more affluent part of the city than the previous house, and I was enamored with it immediately. The home was listed for sale by the owners, so there was no real estate company involved. Thus I made up the purchase agreement myself and presented it. One of its conditions stated that my house on East Campbell Court had to sell previous to my buying the new one. Fortunately the owners accepted the terms of the agreement almost immediately. Consequently I listed my house with my friend, Frank, who was a salesman for a local real estate company. He immediately set about the task of getting it sold.

Within a month Frank found a prospective buyer. After some haggling about the price and a few other details concerning the purchase, we came to an agreement on the sale of the house. Only then did I apply for a loan on the home that I was buying. It was quickly approved and we set a date for the closing. Meanwhile, Frank and the prospective buyers also had set a date for the closing on my house on East Campbell Court. Everything appeared to be progressing smoothly.

Two days before the scheduled closing for the house that I was selling, Frank called and asked to meet with me.

His news was bad. He informed me that there was a problem with the owners, Mr. and Mrs. Cline, from whom I had purchased the house five years ago. It seems that there was a discrepancy between what I owed them on the land contract and what they owed the bank which held their mortgage for the house. I was floored! How could that happen, I wondered.

The explanation was simple though the solution to it was not. During the past five years I had been paying the Clines the contracted monthly amount *plus* an additional $150 each month because I wished to pay off the loan more quickly than the contract called for. Apparently they had been pocketing the extra money and were paying their bank only the regular monthly payment. The net result was that they owed the bank a sum which was five thousand dollars *more* than what I owed them on the house.

The bizarre story seemed even more grotesque when I learned the rest of its details. After selling the house to me the Clines had purchased another in Port Huron—about a hundred miles distant from Midland. Somewhat later they separated and went through divorce proceedings. Currently, Mr. Cline, who had lost his job and was thus unemployed, was living in an apartment somewhere in the Detroit area and Mrs. Cline, with their two children, were living in the Port Huron house and being supported by welfare payments. The house was listed for sale with a real estate company. However, the Port Huron area was suffering layoffs caused by recent plant closings so the city was a depressed area and real estate was not moving at the time. Those facts made it obvious that the two could not come up with the five thousand plus dollars which their bank required to release the house in order for me to sell it to my prospective buyers. What a convoluted muddle!

All progress on both house transactions—the one I was selling as well as the one I was buying—came to an immediate halt. The two house closings had to be postponed—perhaps forever. I had a dreadful sinking feeling in my depths that both deals would fall through without a miracle of some kind. That moribund state of affairs lasted for about two weeks while my salesman friend, Frank, frantically searched for a solution.

Finally, on a dark and overcast day, which fit the occasion perfectly, Frank stopped in to see me. He indicated that after much deliberation he had come up with an idea that possibly could solve the difficulty, but it would depend entirely on me! I didn't much like the sound of that but indicated that I would hear him out anyway. Frank's plan called for me to add five thousand dollars to the amount of the loan I was borrowing for the house I wanted to buy. Then I would loan that money to the Clines in return for a second mortgage of that same amount on their Port Huron house. They could then pay off their bank and the house on East Campbell Court would be released so I could sell it to the prospective buyers. My second mortgage on their Port Huron home would be paid off if or when the house was sold.

The plan would mean that the monthly payments for my new house would be higher, and I would also be the holder of a second mortgage on a house in Port Huron that I had never even seen. Plus, that house was for sale in a seriously lopsided buyer's market where houses were not selling at all. Such a deal, I thought cynically. At least Frank had given me something to mull over anyway. I did just that for about a week before calling him and reluctantly agreeing to the proposal.

Over the next few days all of the following took place in rapid succession. My loan was approved for the higher amount, I in turn loaned the five thousand dollars to the Clines who immediately applied it to their loan on the East Campbell Court house. The bank released that house and I had a closing on it with my prospective buyers. I closed on my new house and moved in almost immediately.

Later I had many misgivings about whether or not I had done the right thing. I relieved my anxiety a bit by driving to Port Huron to at least look at the house of which I was then a part owner and thus prove to myself that it did exist. For a few years I would call Mrs. Cline annually to see if the house had sold or if there were any changes in her financial situation. She was very pleasant and apologized over and over again for the problem. I really believe that she hated getting those calls but never indicated such. Eventually I gave up ever getting any of my money back and ceased bothering her. Much earlier I had already resigned myself to the fact that her ex-husband, Mr. Cline, was a total deadbeat financially, so I didn't even contact him.

Then, after somewhat over ten years had elapsed, I was surprised when an envelope from Mrs. Cline appeared in my mailbox. In her enclosed letter she asked for the exact amount that was owed to me including interest. I called her with the information and was pleased to learn that in the interim she had completed an associate's degree in college. Ironically, at the time she was employed as a consultant in a debt reduction type of business. She had taken her house off the market and was ready to pay off the loan to me. Soon thereafter, a check for the correct sum, which by that time amounted to over twelve thousand dollars, arrived in the mail along with the papers for the second mortgage on the Port Huron house. I happily signed off on it and returned them to Mrs. Cline with a letter explaining how pleased I was over the gratifying conclusion of our extremely unorthodox financial dealings. Happy endings occur not only in movies but occasionally in real life as well.

Chapter Nine

Torch This Place!

In 1981, a little less than five years before I retired from teaching, my housemate, and I visited a couple of friends near Tekonsha, Michigan. The pair, Bob and Dean, had bought a small farm of approximately twenty acres a few miles north of the Indiana/Michigan border. The farm buildings included a small barn, a huge tool shed, an old milk house and a two story four square style house from the early 1900s. I was raised on a farm in rural Michigan so the structures filled me with nostalgia. Bob and Dean had taken the already enchanting older buildings and made them even more so with their imaginative renovations.

They remodeled the small barn into a five room rental unit, the tool shed into a furniture stripping and refinishing business plus an antique furniture and clock shop. The tiny milk house on a circular driveway behind the main house became a quaint potting shed and garden storage building.

The real *piece de résistance*, however, was what they did to the four square style farmhouse. It began as seven rooms and one bath and, after being enlarged in all four directions, became a veritable mansion encompassing ten rooms and two and a half bathrooms. They also added a circular drive leading up to a dramatic new two story porch with tall white columns When the renovations were complete the magnificent home looked as though it had been transplanted intact from the movie, "Gone with the Wind." One would expect Vivian Leigh and Clark Gable to canter up the drive on horseback at any moment.

During our visit, Bob and Dean showed us another house which they were remodeling at the time. It was a Lilliputian Victorian home on the outskirts of Tekonsha. With only three tiny rooms plus a bathroom, it was like a period doll house. When the transformation was finished it would become their third rental unit.

Talking with Bob and Dean about their house projects that weekend was a real eye opener for me. They filled my imagination with all sorts of possibilities and started my remodeling juices flowing in new directions never taken in the past. Because of their inspiration I did my first total house remodeling. Only a couple of years later, I began working on another old house. Within the next ten years I remodeled four more entire houses, adding each of them to my stable of rental units. But that is getting ahead of my story.

A week after my visit with Bob and Dean, I contacted a real estate salesman acquaintance and asked if his company had any small, "junker" type houses for sale. I explained that during my free time I planned to spend the next few months revamping the place. I emphasized that the house must be in poor shape and severely in need of a great deal of tender loving care. Within a week, Jerry, the salesman, came through brilliantly. He called and said he had a prospect for me to look at and consider purchasing.

I met Jerry at the house on Montrose Street and had my initial viewing of what was to become the subject of my first "total house" remodeling project. It was, indeed, in very sad shape, but with good reason. The approximately nine hundred square foot house made up the bulk of an estate which had been owned by an elderly couple. They were physically unable do the necessary basic maintenance for the last few years that they lived. Consequently the sad derelict was in dreadful condition; conversely, it was absolutely ideal for my purposes. Excitedly, I questioned Jerry about the price. It was only $11,000! In that place and time even the tiniest house could bring $20,000 to $25,000. I didn't quibble and immediately signed a purchase agreement which offered the full asking price on a land contract. The deceased couple's son, who was in charge of their estate, accepted the offer and agreed to a $1,500 down payment and monthly contract payments of only $75.00.

When the necessary papers were signed, I became the proud owner of what was probably the epitome of dilapidated houses in the entire city. As a sample of its deplorable condition, not one of the four exterior doors had a workable lock. Almost immediately I secured all of them with padlocks. Upon reflection that was probably wasted effort because what self respecting robber would make the effort to break into such an ignoble heap?

The following weekend I decided to show off the new purchase to Ron, my housemate, and a couple, Jack and Toni, who were friends from the school where I taught. Toni's reaction was the most vivid. She literally turned green as she walked across the filthy rags of carpeting and into the kitchen which had strings of grease hanging from the ceiling like stalactites in a cave. Toni abruptly brought the tour to an end and insisted that Jack and she go home, where, they told me later, she became violently ill.

Ron's reaction, though not quite so dramatic, was nonetheless very succinct. He looked through the house from stem to stern, including the living room, two bedrooms, dining room, kitchen, bathroom, sun porch and even the damp basement where one could hear water dripping constantly. He turned to me and said most emphatically, "Torch this place!"

Undaunted, I eagerly started the remodeling project by hiring a city truck for hauling debris to the local landfill. Most of the rooms on the first floor were nearly empty, but the four hundred square foot partial basement under the rear half of the house was crammed to overflowing. Much personal family memorabilia and bushels of refuse were left there by the unfortunate former owners. In a very short time the back of the dump truck was filled, all my muscles were aching, and I hadn't even begun the demolition part of the remodeling project yet!

After the house was empty, I found that I was better able to view the situation and make renovation plans. The pitiful house was rife with serious problems. Numbered among them were: It needed a new interior layout because the present one was totally unworkable. A sagging roof at the rear of the house indicated that there were support problems. All the plumbing in the kitchen and bathroom needed replacing. In fact, I discovered that the bathtub was draining directly into a vile-smelling pond in the crawl space under the front of the house. The house needed an entirely new furnace system including ductwork. It was being heated by two wall-furnace space heaters—neither of which was operable at the time of purchase. The man I called to check the furnaces said he wouldn't light either of them for fear of causing an explosion. The outmoded knob and tube wiring came up far short of code requirements. All the electrical components, as well as the service panel had to be updated. The panel consisted of a sixty amp fuse box with only four fuses, indicating there were only four circuits in the entire structure.

The situation on the exterior of the house was equally as grim. The roof had to be re-shingled as there were leaks here and there throughout the house. One of them, near the side entrance, resulted in a minor Niagara Falls spilling down the wall during each heavy rainstorm. Behind the house, near the back fence, stood the macabre skeleton of a long dead tree. The lawn was merely a collection of dandelions and other assorted weeds. Much of the property was ringed with overgrown shrubbery and the

sidewalk to the front door had deteriorated into a few broken pieces of cement. The eave troughs and downspouts
were rusted out tatters of their former selves. Finally, the
asbestos shingles used as siding were filthy and painted a
dull gray. Many of them were broken thus requiring re-
moval and replacement.

Initially I was in a quandary about where to begin
because there was so much revamping to do. After weeks of
deliberation I came up with two plans. The first was a rough
schedule where I listed the main items to be worked on and
the approximate order in which I would tackle each of them.
At that juncture I had little or no idea of how long the renovation would take.

The second plan was a before and after scale drawing of the home's layout. (See the floor plans at the end of
this chapter.) As I mentioned already, there were a number
of room arrangement or layout problems, the most prominent of which were: There were four exterior doors in all.
One was on the front of the house and led into the living
room. The second was on the driveway and led into the side
entrance. A third was at grade level in the rear. That was the
one and only access to the basement level. The fourth exterior door was also at the rear of the house and led from a
rickety set of steps made of un-mortared cement blocks, into
the sun porch. It is my contention that no house of only nine
hundred square feet needs any more than two exterior doors.

The next layout problem was that the bedrooms were
widely separated from one another and from the bathroom.
For example in order to go from the front bedroom to the

bathroom, one had to traverse a virtual maze. To further illustrate my concern, let's take an imaginary nighttime visit to the bathroom. Starting in the bedroom, it required going into the living room, turning right and going into the dining room, making another right into the side entrance where a final right turn would bring the person to the bathroom. Looking at the floor plan one observes that the bedroom and bathroom are immediately adjacent to one another but, because of the room arrangement, it was almost a case of "you can't get there from here."

An additional room arrangement problem was that it was necessary to go outside the house in order to enter the basement. I planned to have a hookup for the washer and dryer in that part of the house, therefore the access problem would be nearly impossible—especially considering frigid Michigan winters.

Surprisingly the entire house contained one lonely closet. It was a walk through type between the back bedroom and the side entrance and it had only four feet of hanging space. Of course, in the present age, that is inadequate for any house, small or large.

The final layout difficulty was that there were windows from the sun porch into the kitchen and the back bedroom. In my plans I assumed the sun porch could serve as a possible guest bedroom thus, to ensure a little privacy; those extra windows had to go.

The "After" house plan at the end of this chapter shows clearly how all of the room arrangement difficulties were solved. First I removed the closet between the back bedroom and the side entrance. That made an L shaped room which would serve as the new living room and dining room. Near the side door, which became the new main entrance, I erected a wall divider and entry closet, and thus created a small foyer.

Next I tackled the old living room which, in combination with the bathroom and the small front bedroom, became the new sleeping wing of the house. A newly positioned archway led from the dining room into a hallway, which in turn provided access to the two bedrooms and a small linen closet. The original bathroom door was closed up and relocated off that hallway as well. To provide space for opening the new bathroom door, it was necessary to exchange the locations of the toilet and sink in the bathroom. The bathtub remained in its original position. For each bedroom I found room enough for a good sized closet and enclosed each of them with bi-fold doors.

A look at the "after" floor plan may show the careful observer that the added walls for the closets and hallway are not as thick as the original walls. The reason is that I wanted to save space. Consequently I set the framing 2 by 4s the narrow way in the new walls I built. That made them about three instead of six inches thick—even tiny inches counted in such a cramped situation.

By the time all those interior alterations were finished, the winter was giving way to warm spring weather so I could move some of my operations outside. I put a large new window in the relocated living room, removed the old porch and door from the front of the house, replaced the windows in what were now the two front bedrooms and ex-changed the single window in the dining room for a larger picture window. Of course those renovations messed up the exterior siding considerably so I replaced it wherever neces-sary before turning my attention to the back part of the house.

At the rear of the house the major problems involved the extra back door in the sun porch and the basement stair-way which allowed entrance only from the outside. First I took down the wall separating the sun porch and the base-ment stairway. Next I cut back the sun porch floor enough to add four steps and then reinforced the floor structure. I built the new steps to lead from the sun porch down to the grade entrance. From that level one could either turn right and go on down into the basement or turn left and go out to the back yard.

That was one more problem solved, and the bonus effect was that the new direct access from the sun porch to the back yard via the stairs made the sun porch door redun-dant. Originally that wall of the sun porch had two single windows on each side of the door. After removing the doorway, I resituated the window nearest the basement stair in the spot the door had occupied. The result was an unbro-ken tier of four single windows across the back wall of the sun porch. After removing the unwanted windows leading into the new living room and the kitchen, then I built a closet for the sun porch in the L shaped corner formed by the basement stairway.

That latter project completed the interior structural changes which I was capable of accomplishing without professional assistance. The house renovation, however, was far from being completed. I hired a friend to replace all the kitchen and bathroom plumbing and to exchange the two wall heaters for a single, larger furnace in the basement. (See the chapter called "The Wizard of Plumbing and Heating.)

I hired an electrician to replace the fuse box with a 200 amp service panel which had breaker switches instead of the older style fuses. Several other friends helped me tear the multiple layers of old shingles off the roof, repair the broken boards we found there and then put new asphalt shingles in place. We started very early each morning while doing that job because the heat from the sun later in the day radiated up from the shingles making it nearly unbearable. For their hard work under nearly impossible conditions, I still owe a big debt of gratitude to those wonderful friends. Another loyal friend helped me with the dirty job of blowing insulation into the attic cavity. That occurred after I had propped up and strengthened the sagging roof.

There had been a rickety porch on the front of the house. It was no longer in use because I had removed the old front door. I got rid of the porch by dismantling the roof and rails, breaking up the cement base with a sledge hammer and carting the debris in trailer load after trailer load to the city landfill.

When the reconstruction was all finished, the house still lacked curb appeal. That was changed dramatically when I painted the entire house a warm chocolate brown with white trim around the windows. Then I designed and built cream colored, cottage-style wooden shutters. After removing the skeleton of the old dead tree from the back fence line, I trimmed the overgrown bushes back, reseeded the lawn, and transplanted small evergreens across the front of the house. Then I put in a ground level back door step and built a new sidewalk to replace the old broken one leading to the street. The once forlorn house had been transformed from the ugly duckling of the neighborhood to a veritable swan.

I could go on and on describing all the tasks, both large and small, required to bring the forlorn house on Montrose Street back to life once again. They were too numerous for a complete listing in this limited chapter and likely it would take an entire book to do them full justice. The total remodel took about fifteen months. During much of that year I was also teaching and thus only able to spend evenings, weekends and, of course, the summer on the project. I should add, however, that the hundreds of hours spent on that renovation likely were the most satisfying I have ever experienced. Each day, after school, I would hurry home, change my clothing, and rush to the other house. I looked forward with eager anticipation to every weekend when I was able to spend entire days there. My social life dwindled but my personal fulfillment grew correspondingly.

I fully intended to sell the house after it was remodeled. But, before I was halfway through, I knew that was going to be impossible for me. So much of the "inner me" had gone into the renovation that it would be nearly the same as selling one of my arms or legs, therefore I had to come up with another plan for its use.

Remodeling the house had yet another long-term effect for me. The project gave me the idea for how I would like to spend at least a portion of my time after I retired from teaching. Three years later, in 1986, I did retire at the age of fifty-three. The summer after that I bought another forlorn "junker" house and when my former colleagues returned to work in the fall, I happily began its renovation. A carload of those fellow teachers came to the new project that first day of school to facetiously "console" me about not returning to teaching. They went away with the realization that there was no happier retiree than I was.

MONTROSE STREET HOUSE REMODEL
Midland, Michigan – 1982

BEFORE

AFTER

MONTROSE STREET HOUSE REMODEL
Midland, Michigan – 1982

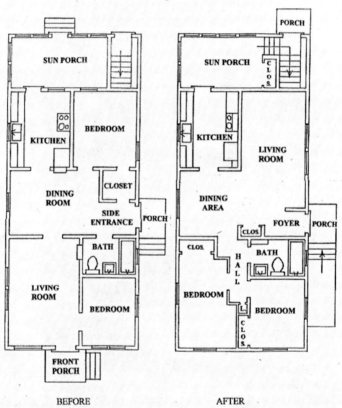

BEFORE   AFTER

Chapter Ten

The Wizard of Plumbing and Heating

The total house remodel I discussed in the chapter called "Torch This Place" would have been completely impossible for me without the invaluable help of one very special person. He is a master craftsman named Bill McGregor and was a major player in all the remodeling projects that I undertook from 1982 until I moved to New Mexico over a decade later. I think that he richly deserves an entire chapter in any book about my activities in the field of renovation.

I met Bill through his wife, Marianne, who was a teacher's aide, or paraprofessional, at Central Intermediate School where I taught from 1968 until I retired in 1986. Our meeting came about as a result of yet another remodeling project. A year or so after I bought my first house in Midland, I decided to remodel the unfinished basement in the residence. It was my intention to update about half of that little-used space into a family room with a small kitchenette/wet bar, a bedroom and a three-piece bathroom.

Marianne heard me talking about my new project in the school cafeteria and, in an offhand way, wondered who would be doing the plumbing for the job. I had no one in mind and asked if she had any suggestions. She said that her husband, Bill, worked full time for a plumbing and heating contractor in town but that he often "moonlighted" by taking on private jobs for other people. Needless to say, I was very interested because, though I could do many types of renovation work, plumbing was like an indecipherable foreign language to me. It was obvious to me that I was far out of my depth in that regard so I questioned Marianne further about her husband and his "extra curricular" plumbing jobs.

A few evenings later Marianne brought Bill to my house so we could meet one another and, more importantly, so he could see what I had in mind for the remodeling project in the basement. I saw immediately that "Mac," as he was nicknamed, was a fascinating character. His short, very thickly built body supported an enormous head of curly red hair that was beginning to go gray. He spoke in abbreviated, choppy sentences but each word he employed was full of significance. That evening he summed up the plumbing field for me in one short sentence. According to Mac, this was the essence of his chosen line of endeavor. "Hot water is on the left, cold water is on the right, shit does not run uphill and payday is on Thursday."

That first meeting was prophetic in yet another way. Over the next ten years or so, Marianne would often accompany Bill when he worked on various remodeling projects for me. She always seemed perfectly content to watch television in the family room or living room while he and I worked on whatever project was underway at the time. I had to agree with her that doing so likely would be more interesting to her than spending the evening at home alone.

Mac taught me much about plumbing and later, about heating as well. Not that he had me operating the soldering iron or actually doing the pipe fitting, but instead he showed me what I could do to get everything prepared in advance for him so that he wasn't required to waste valuable time on things that I, an amateur, could just as easily accomplish. Mac's tutelage in plumbing and heating reminded me much of when I had worked as an electrician's helper for Temple's Electric Shop in Vassar while I was in college. I was there mainly to facilitate the expert in the field but, as a bonus, managed to learn a great deal about what we were doing. For example, when Mac and I worked on that first project, I would prepare the way for him by breaking up the cement floor where new plumbing was to go and he could then get to it immediately during the time he was there. I carefully watched each of his efficient moves and increased my own knowledge by doing so.

Mac also inspired me with the necessary confidence to go on to bigger and better remodeling projects. Merely knowing that he would be there to help me with the plumbing and heating areas of renovation, gave me the necessary nerve to tackle all of the larger projects that I did over the next few years.

During the year that I worked on my first total house renovation, Mac put in a new forced air furnace and added ductwork throughout the house. (See the chapter called "Torch This Place!") You will probably recall that the house had formerly been heated with two wall furnaces and consequently no ductwork had been necessary. In the plumbing area, Mac replaced all the outdated hot and cold water and drainage piping for the bathroom and kitchen. In the basement he installed a new water heater, a washer and dryer hookup, and a sump pump for keeping the basement dry.

There seemed to be no limitations on what Mac was able to do in the areas of plumbing and heating. All I had to do was show him the rough plans for what I had in mind for renovations and he immediately began his magic. He was especially instrumental, even essential, when I did my third total house renovation. In fact that project on Hines Street in Midland turned out to be the largest undertaking we did together. The house had two apartments—the larger one originally contained a living room, dining area, kitchen, a bathroom and four bedrooms plus basement storage. The smaller flat was what is usually referred to as a "mother-in-law" apartment with a living room, kitchen, bedroom, bathroom and also some basement storage.

I tackled the larger apartment first with big plans. On the second floor I renovated two of the bedrooms into a master suite with its own combination walk-in closet/dressing room and master bath. (See the Before and After house plans at the end of this chapter.) Because that bathroom originally had been the only one in the apartment, I added another one off the hallway to serve the other two bedrooms. Mac replaced the sink and toilet in the master bath and did all the plumbing for the new hallway bath as well. That job necessitated my removing the ceiling of the kitchen below so he could add the necessary water lines and the new drains. When we moved downstairs, he also replaced the sink in the kitchen and added a dishwasher as well. In the basement he installed two water heaters and two washer and dryer hookups—one of each for the two units.

Later we turned to the heating problems. Originally both units had been heated by an enormous out-dated gas forced air furnace. The only thermostatic control was in the larger apartment which meant that the people in the smaller apartment were at the mercy of their neighbors for heat control. In my estimation that was an untenable situation and I determined to change it. My solution was to divide the ductwork and put in two new furnaces—a big one for the larger unit and a smaller one for the mother-in-law apartment. Mac agreed that my solution was possible and set to work on it. While he was dividing the complicated maze of ductwork, I attacked the old furnace. It was simply too large to haul up the stairs in one unit so I took it apart, piece by piece, and was able to remove it in that fashion.

After the larger unit was remodeled and it was rented to a tenant, I began work on renovating the interior of the mother-in-law apartment. Mac was essential there too. I wanted to re-arrange the kitchen counters and cupboards so there would be room for a small eat-in area. That necessitated removing a large window in addition to changing the locations of all the appliances including the sink, the range and the refrigerator. Mac tore out the old sink, did the new piping for the water and drain lines, and then installed the new kitchen sink. He left his indelible mark in the bathroom for that unit also by putting in a different sink and toilet. By the time we were finished Mac had been instrumental in altering every part of both units in the house. (See the Before and After floor plans at the end of this chapter.)

During the time I was writing this chapter, I mentally totaled all the projects that Mac helped me with during the decade plus that we worked together. Here they are: He added two complete bathrooms and two half baths where none existed previously. He remodeled the plumbing or added plumbing to eight additional bathrooms. He installed five washer and dryer hookups, eight new hot water heaters and one entire house air conditioning unit. He remodeled the plumbing in six different kitchens, plus he installed three dishwashers and four garbage disposals. He installed four new complete furnaces and did the total ductwork for one of those and also divided the ductwork leading from two of the others. Is it any wonder that I refer to Mac as "The Wizard of Plumbing and Heating?"

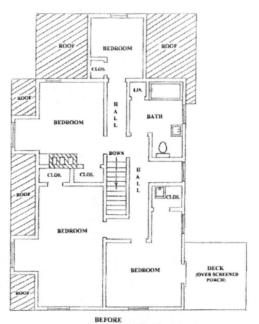

HINES STREET HOUSE
SECOND FLOOR REMODEL
Midland, Michigan – 1990

BEFORE

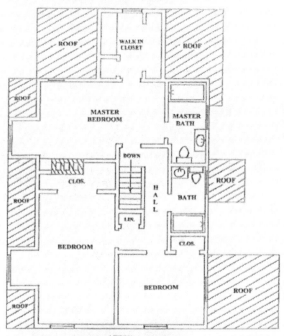

HINES STREET HOUSE
SECOND FLOOR REMODEL
Midland, Michigan – 1990

AFTER

Chapter Eleven

The Renter from Heaven

After I had spent a year completing my first full-house remodeling, I found that I was so attached to the house that I simply could not part with it. My original intent had been to rehabilitate the home and then sell it for a profit before going on to another one of the same sort. I planned the project to be a sort of precursor to the present-day television show called "Flip That House," though that show was unheard of in 1985 and 1986 when I was doing my "flip." At the completion of the renovation, however, my feelings did not allow me to follow my intended course of action. Something in my warped imagination told me that selling the house would be tantamount to selling a child and that was an anathema to me.

Because I was unable or unwilling to sell the house, apparently the only remaining avenue open to me, was to rent it to a tenant. That action, too, gave me serious pause. Renters, in general, have poor reputations in the area of home maintenance. For the most part they seem lack the ability or willingness to give a home or an apartment the tender loving care that it requires. I was immediately reminded of an apartment where I had stayed a few nights while working on my master's degree at Central Michigan University in 1968 and 1969. Except on special occasions, I was a commuting student driving back and forth each day from Saginaw, where I lived, to Mt. Pleasant, where the university was located.

Exam week during the university summer sessions was one of the times when I occasionally stayed overnight in Mt. Pleasant. That gave me more time for studying. I heard of an apartment where one could rent a room for a single night and decided to investigate. When I went to view the room, to my surprise, I discovered that the building was a rather new one and looked quite presentable from the outside. But, as soon as I entered the individual unit, that was no longer the case. The students who lived there during the regular school year had done a thorough job of trashing the apartment. The furniture was broken and filthy, the walls were scarred and the carpeting was dirt encrusted and in tatters. By nature I am a rather fastidious individual, so to me the entire place was a pig sty and nearly uninhabitable. However, the price was relatively low and I only planned to spend a few nights there, so with clenched teeth, I agreed to pay the asked for rental amount.

I had visions of that same sort of disaster happening to my own "flip" house where I had spent a little over a year and a lot of money making profound and far-reaching improvements. Those efforts had the desired effect because they changed the dilapidated house into a little gem of a cottage. I was very proud of it and of all the improvements that had been made. It probably would break my heart if I saw the house revert to its former unhappy condition. Practicality, however, won out in my internal war and I decided, against my better judgment, to give landlordism a temporary try.

Reluctantly I put an advertisement in the local newspaper and awaited results. They came almost immediately. Many people were interested enough to tour the house and very often their reaction was, "This is the nicest rental house on the market." The prospective renters' responses pleased me very much and they calmed my fears to an extent. I surmised that if the tenants initially found the house in immaculate order, perhaps it would encourage them to leave it in a similar condition when their leases were fulfilled.

One of the prospective renters who viewed the house was a Mrs. Carris. I had met her previously because her older daughter had been one of my American history students at Central Intermediate School a few years before. By that time the daughter was a senior in high school. Mr. Carris was an employee of Dow Chemical Company, which is headquartered in Midland, but he was on temporary assignment in the Union of South Africa. During the year of her husband's stay in Africa, Mrs. Carris and their two daughters planned to rent a house. Then the family would buy a permanent home once Mr. Carris returned from overseas.

I liked the Carrises very much and chose them to be my initial renters. Fortunately their plans meshed with my own perfectly. I was reluctant to enter into a long-term rental agreement because, as far as I was concerned, my being a landlord was on a trial basis. Together we negotiated a rental contract wherein the Carrises were to pay a refundable $300.00 damage deposit plus the $300.00 first month's rent at the time of the contract signing. That was agreeable to them as well. All went smoothly with the signing and the Carrises soon moved into the house. "Perhaps," I mused hopefully, "being a landlord will not turn into a catastrophe after all."

When the Carrises had rented the house for less than a month, they asked if I would erect some sort of storage building in the back yard where they could keep their lawnmower and other yard and garden tools. As things then existed, they were forced to store the mower in the basement and Mrs. Carris and her daughters had a problem hauling it up and down the stairway each time it was used. I was already feeling bereft without a house to remodel in my spare time, so I was happy, and even eager, to comply. I had lot of fun designing and erecting the little building. (See the photographs of the storage building at the end of this chapter.) "Well," I thought, "being a landlord was turning out to be very pleasant, indeed."

As the due date for the second month's rent rolled around, Mrs. Carris, as expected, promptly presented me with the check. Later, at home, I looked at it and realized that instead of its amount being the agreed-upon $300.00, it was made out for $350.00. "What was going on?" I wondered. I called Mrs. Carris and asked about it. She explained that during her search for a house she and a friend had toured a great number of rental homes in the city and she decided that I was not charging a high enough rent for the house. Thus she had arbitrarily raised it by fifty dollars per month. I was astounded! Until that time I had very little experience with tenants and rental houses, but nonetheless I felt the action was unheard of in the annals of landlordism.

From that day forward all of the rental checks included the extra fifty dollars. In fact, during that time, even I apparently became a believer because, when I put the advertisement in the newspaper at the end of the Carrises' lease period, I quoted the monthly rent as being $350.00. If Mrs. Carris felt that was a fair rent for the house, who was I to disagree with her?

My relations with the Carrises stayed extremely cordial during their entire tenure in the house. In fact when I did maintenance work on the property, usually they invited me in for coffee or snacks. They were fun to be with and I enjoyed them thoroughly. The entire family treated the house and grounds with the utmost respect and left it in the same good repair that they initially found it.

Something a bit amusing did occur just prior to their moving at the end of the lease period. Mrs. Carris approached me and said that she suspected the elder daughter had somehow ruined the lock on the bathroom door. She indicated that I should take some money out of the damage deposit for replacing it. Upon examining the lock I learned that it only needed a little oil to make it work smoothly again. Nothing was broken. In no time the lock was oiled and working well and of course no charge had to be levied against the deposit.

When Mr. Carris returned from Africa at the year's end, the couple purchased a home just as they had planned. They gave me the required one month's notice prior to their projected move to the new house. I found that my only distress about their leaving was that a very pleasant experience was coming to a close. Their taking leave of the rental house did not actually end our relationship, however. After the move across town, they invited me to the new house to visit and I did so a number of times.

In retrospect, I must say that at the end of that contract, I had nothing negative to relate about my first experience as a landlord. In fact it was a delight from start to finish. None of the horror stories I had either imagined or heard about came to pass during my own start into the new business venture. "Maybe most renters are like the Carrises." I thought to myself. My confidence had risen to new heights and I was actually looking forward to the next experience with eager anticipation. Little did I know or suspect what fate had in store for me.

STORAGE SHED
MONTROSE HOUSE
MIDLAND, MICHIGAN - 1986

Chapter Twelve

The Renter from the "Other Place"

My very first experience at being a landlord did not adequately prepare me for what was to occur during the second experience. In fact, Mrs. Carris, the first renter, lulled me into a false sense of security by encouraging me to think that all renters would fit into the same mold. Mrs. Carris's kind and thoughtful actions showed that she thought of me, her landlord, first and foremost in all of our dealings. (See the chapter called "The Renter From Heaven.") The second renter, Mrs. Doyle, was a horse of a different color. In fact she became "The Renter From Hell."

The clean up process after Mrs. Carris ended her contract and moved out was a very short one because she and her family left the house in nearly pristine condition. Therefore, in almost no time, I placed an advertisement in the local newspaper announcing the house's availability for another tenant. The first person to answer the ad was a pleasant and very sweet lady named Mrs. Doyle whom I knew already because her older son had been one of my students. The story she told about her reasons for needing a house to rent was an entirely legitimate and believable one. It seems that after Mr. Doyle died, she could no longer manage the paint store that the two of them owned so she put it on the market and it soon passed into other hands. The couple had lived in a large house near the center of town and since she had only one child living with her (a boy of nineteen) she wanted to move to a smaller place. She claimed that she recently sold that home and indicated that my small rental would be ideal for the two of them.

In my Never Never Land naivety Mrs. Doyle seemed as though she would be the ideal renter. She told me her income included the proceeds from the sale of her home and the paint store plus a monthly Social Security check. Thus her finances seemed secure. As an added bonus, I had become well acquainted with her when the son had been my student. Our dealings had always been pleasant and no problems had arisen during that entire school year. I felt that everything boded well for a pleasant tenant/landlord relationship and looked forward to it.

Just over a week later Mrs. Doyle and I met to sign the rental contract. According to its provisions she was to pay a $300 damage fee plus $350 for the first month's rent at the time of the signing. At that point I had my first clue that all was not well and that there was trouble on the horizon. Mrs. Doyle appeared at the meeting with a check for $350 only. She apologized profusely and said there had been some minor problem with her latest Social Security check and that she would get the damage deposit to me the very next week. Hindsight now tells me that I should have ended the deal right then, but I didn't. You have probably heard the old adage that states unequivocally, "Hindsight is better than foresight by a damned sight, and that is an insight." I ignored the profound wisdom of that saying and allowed Mrs. Doyle and her son to move into the rental after paying only the first month's rent.

Likely you have already figured out what eventually happened. To my chagrin, Mrs. Doyle *never* paid the damage fee and the next rent payment she made was not until six months later! But, I'm getting ahead of my story.

A week after Mrs. Doyle and her son moved into the rental, I visited them to pick up the promised check. Once again she was most apologetic in saying that she still hadn't received her money from the Social Security Administration and asked that I come back again the next week. That went on for an entire month by which time the second monthly rent check was due. When I attempted to collect it Mrs. Doyle explained that her husband's death had left the Social Security account in a mess and she had received a check for only fifty dollars which was supposed to last her through the month. Of course, consequently, she would be unable to pay the rent. Another month went by and her excuse that time was that the Social Security office which served Midland (where we lived) was in Saginaw, twenty-five miles away, and it was open for business to Midland residents only on Wednesday mornings. Since she had no automobile, Mrs. Doyle explained that it was difficult for her to be in Saginaw at the proper time.

Yet another month went by and neither the security deposit nor any of the rent money appeared. By that time the lady owed me a total of $1,350 and I was so frustrated that I was ready to tear my hair out by the roots. Finally, in exasperation, I told her that I would be at the house the very next Wednesday at 8:00 a.m. sharp in order to take her to Saginaw. I warned her to be ready when I got there. True to my promise, I appeared at the designated time on the designated Wednesday. Mrs. Doyle came to the door and I asked her if she were set to travel. Instead of answering she handed me a check for $350. Apparently, by some sort of magic or voodoo, some of her Social Security money had arrived! I asked for the rest of the money she owed but was told that she didn't have it.

Tired of being "Mr. Nice Guy" and being trod on unscrupulously because of it, I announced that I was immediately going to the Court House to file an eviction notice on Mrs. Doyle for failure to pay the rent. I did so and roughly a month later there was a hearing scheduled during which she was going to have a chance to answer the charge. Of course, she was unable to do so, therefore the judge ruled that she must vacate the premises in two weeks. With his ruling, I thought that my major problems with "The Renter From Hell" were over, but unfortunately they were just getting underway.

On the afternoon prior the day Mrs. Doyle was to be out of the house, an attorney phoned me. He said that he was appealing on her behalf. He asked that because she couldn't be out of the house by the next day, she be allowed to stay through the following weekend. Grudgingly, I granted his request. However, taking no chances, I made

certain that I was at the rental house by 8:00 a.m. the following Monday.

Mrs. Doyle and her son were, indeed, gone but they
left total chaos behind them. The little house—which had
been immaculate only six months previously—was filled
with a mountain of trash. Every room was strewn with food
containers (many with rotting food still in them), there were
piles of wadded scrap paper throughout the house, the carpeting and floor tiles in every room had huge stains, the
walls, even those that were paneled, were smudged and
filthy, the toilet, sink and tub in the bathroom appeared
never to have been cleaned and there was even a mysterious
little pile of congealed jam on the tile floor near the toilet.
The kitchen appliances were grease encrusted and the cupboards were unbelievable filthy and filled with junk. The
back entrance and the basement fared no better than the
other rooms as they had trash, including broken furniture,
cardboard boxes and discarded clothing strewn from wall to
wall. During the clean-up process over the next few weeks, I
filled thirty-six large plastic leaf bags to the brim with debris from the inside of the tiny nine hundred square foot
house.

When I went out to the back yard to survey the situation there, my heart plummeted. Mrs. Doyle had erected a
large, olive drab army tent covering about a third of the
small yard behind the house. In the tent she had stored
boxes of home-canned fruits, meats and vegetables. Hundreds of the food items were in sealed glass jars which shat-
tered when left outdoors throughout the extremely cold
Michigan winter in which nighttime temperatures often

dropped below zero. Mixed in amongst the aggregate of broken glass were rotting raspberries, strawberries, peaches, beets, string beans, green peas, dill pickles, apples, pears, ham slices, chicken pieces and dozens of other foods. The odor was overwhelming.

Later, in an almost vain attempt to clean up the disgusting accumulation, I hired a city-owned truck and parked it in the driveway as near to the tent as possible. Then a group of friends and I tried to fold and lift the tent in one piece onto the truck, with all the broken jars of food inside. That plan failed miserably. The liquids had rotted the heavy fabric of the tent floor and when we lifted it on to the truck, the entire offensive jumble of broken glass and food particles streamed through the holes to the ground leaving an even more disgusting soup behind.

The problem was only partially solved later when I raked the debris into piles, shoveled it into metal containers and hauled it to the disposal grounds. Hundreds of tiny fragments of glass were still left in the topsoil. Most of those I removed by gathering them individually while spending many laborious hours on my hands and knees using work gloves and heavy kneepads. The grass which had previously covered that area was long gone so I had a load of topsoil hauled in which I spread across the area before planting new grass. The entire clean up process, inside and out, took nearly two months, during which time the house remained vacant and therefore bringing in no rental income.

I hadn't forgotten that Mrs. Doyle still owed me more than a thousand dollars which I was determined to wrest from her if at all possible. I sued her in the Small

Claims Court and, though the decision was in my favor,
when I asked the Judge how I should go about collecting my
money, he had no practical solution for me. He did say that
the judgment would be in her credit report and, in case she
ever wished to borrow money, it would be a black mark on
her record, but that was of little or no consolation. Twenty-
three years have passed since that hearing and I have never
heard another word about the money from either the court or
Mrs. Doyle.

My experience with the lady I prefer to call "The
Renter From Hell" taught me a number of valuable lessons
about renting houses. I am indebted to Mrs. Doyle who was
my best teacher in the hard knocks school of landlordism.
The first and foremost of those lessons was, do not take any
actions (such as letting them move in) only on the renters'
word that they will pay at a certain time. Get the money
first! Secondly, include a clause in the contract stating that
you, as the landlord, have the right to make inspections, inside and outside the premises, whenever you choose.
Thirdly, do not give a renter any special privileges (such as
late payments, deferring damage deposits or anything involving money) merely because you know them from past
dealings of any sort. Those warnings make me sound as
though I am the opposite of "Mr. Nice Guy" which I prefer
to be in all my dealings but, their importance in tenant-
landlord relations is much greater than my "Nice Guy" repu-
tation. If only I had followed those three simple precepts in
my dealings with Mrs. Doyle, I could have avoided the
trauma during an extremely expensive eight month period of
my life.

Chapter Thirteen

The Mother-in-Law Apartment

The home rental business occupied the major part of my time and energies during the first decade after I retired from teaching. During that period, in addition to the two different houses I lived in, I bought four old houses that were seriously in need of a great deal of tender loving care. I spent roughly a year on each renovating them to a condition where I hoped that they would attract competent and responsible tenants. As a rule most of the units fared reasonably well while being rented out but there were some noteworthy exceptions. (See the chapter called "The Renter from the Other Place!")

The most obvious exception to the above rule was the smallest unit that I owned. That rental seemed to attract only the bottom feeders in the gene pool of tenants. The unit was what is usually called a mother-in-law apartment and it occupied one side of the first floor of a large house that I owned on Hines Street in Midland, Michigan. (See the floor plan at the end of this chapter.) The unit consisted of a living room with a fireplace, a kitchen, a bedroom and a bathroom. It also had access to the basement and one of the two car stalls in the detached garage was assigned to that apartment.

When I first bought the house the larger of the two apartments was empty and I began renovating that part of the unit immediately. The mother-in-law apartment was being rented by a young man in his early twenties. He was single and not very particular about his living conditions, so for the time being I left the unit exactly as it was while I concentrated only on the major apartment.

I made extensive renovations in the larger unit over the next year and at the end of that time was ready to rent it to a tenant. By that time the renter living in the mother-in-law apartment, had made plans to get married and he and his future bride moved into a larger apartment elsewhere in the city. Thus, I was free to renovate the smaller unit in the house.

It took about six months of concentrated effort to bring the small apartment up to my expectations. These are the improvements I made while working on that project.

I remodeled the kitchen by re-arranging the cupboards and removing a window thus allowing space for a small eating area. I re-covered the countertops, added a range hood and installed a new sink in a different location. I also replaced the tiled floor in the kitchen and purchased new appliances. In the living room I repaired the fireplace surround and its glass doors, I patched the damaged plaster, painted the walls and re-carpeted throughout. In the bath-room I replaced the floor tile and the toilet and put in a cabinet type of vanity to take the place of the wall-hung sink. The bedroom required little other than some plaster re-pair, repainting and carpeting.

In the basement I made what were likely the most noteworthy improvements. There I divided the heating sys-tem in order that the mother-in-law apartment would have its own furnace and thermostatic control and in the laundry room I added a separate washer and dryer hookup for that unit. When I was finished, the apartment, though still small, was a gem of a living unit and I was extremely proud of it. (See the photos at the end of this chapter.)

The first tenant in the newly remodeled apartment was a single lady in her thirties. Her credentials all seemed to be in good order. She signed a lease for a year and appar-ently had no problem coming up with the damage deposit and the first month's rent which I required before a tenant moved into any of the units.

Pride of ownership and the desire to see how they were faring, prompted me to drive by all of my rental units frequently. The tenants probably had a vaguely ominous feeling that "Big Brother" was watching them—and he was! A couple of months after the lady moved into the mother-in-law apartment I swung by the house and saw something that disturbed me. The lady was keeping her uncovered trash can and also some cleaning supplies on the tiny front porch that had a door that led into the kitchen as well as another which was the main entrance to the living room. Storing garbage on the exterior of a house without proper containers was not only illegal in Midland, but it also disturbed my own sensibilities. I promptly called the tenant and informed her of such. She readily cooperated by moving the trash to a properly covered container in the garage.

The next difficulty appeared a few months later. I received a call from the tenant informing me that there had been an attempted break-in during which the apartment's front screened door was wrecked. While I was investigating the problem, the lady let it slip that the damage was caused by a boyfriend of hers whom she had allowed into the apartment. "Aha! The plot thickens!" I thought.

I had the door repaired and promptly sent her a bill. She then called me and asked if my house insurance shouldn't pay the cost. I told her that seeing she had freely invited the boyfriend into the apartment, the insurance company claimed that she was responsible and refused to honor the claim. The lady was not very happy about it but she did end up paying the bill.

The next tenant in the mother-in-law apartment was another single lady—probably in her late twenties. She caused me no problems other than the fact that she was forced to break her year long lease after roughly six months because of a job transfer. Unhappily I accepted that state of affairs because I saw no alternative for either of us. I probably would have been even less happy had I been able to foretell what problems I was going to face during the ensuing few months as a direct result of her premature decampment.

An advertisement I placed in the local newspaper put me in contact with the two young people who rented the apartment after that previous renter moved on. They were an unmarried couple, in their early twenties, attending the local college, Northwood Institute. The pair asked for a shorter six month lease on the apartment because they had only that long before the college semester would come to an end. I was a bit reluctant to grant their wish until I met and talked with the boy's parents. The older couple's sincerity encouraged me to rent to the son and his girlfriend. The parents seemed like a responsible, upstanding middle aged pair who had everyone's best interests at heart, including mine. Could a son from such a union cause me serious problems as a landlord? Probably not, I naively reasoned.

The couple moved into the apartment and I heard no disturbances from them while they lived there. As per usual I made my frequent forays driving past the house and saw nothing untoward occurring. All seemed to be progressing well and my worries soon abated. At the end of the college semester the young couple moved out of the house as planned. As I always do when a tenant leaves, I went to inspect the apartment in order to see what needed doing prior to my renting it to another tenant. My mood was unworried and serene.

As soon as I opened the front door and took one quick glance, all my serenity left me. The carpeting, which had been perfect when they moved in, was in tatters and had huge black streaks across it. The fireplace was filled with ashes and the glass doors were soot encrusted. One of them had been smashed and the glass was scattered nearby. The bedroom and living room walls looked as though charcoal had been rubbed into them. Some of the spots were as large as three feet by three feet but I never learned what had caused the discoloration. The shower walls over the tub in the bathroom were black with mildew and both the window curtain and the shower curtain were hanging in shreds. The tub, the toilet and the sink all were encrusted with filth as well.

The kitchen was equally as revolting as the bathroom. The new stainless steel sink was garbage encrusted and the disposal was plugged and consequently not working. There were marks on the walls and dirty fingerprints on most of the cupboard doors. The apartment-sized range was so fully covered with baked on food scraps that it was unrecognizable as the same appliance I had purchased new just a little less than two years previously. Unidentifiable dreck and other debris were ground into both the new floor tile and the carpeting throughout the unit. It was disgusting! If I were to write an entire chapter describing the condition in which I found the apartment, I would probably title it, "From Treasure to Slum in Six Short Months!"

I spent the next month bringing the misused apartment back to its former condition. All the carpeting had to be discarded and replaced with new. I removed the mildew in the bathroom by scrubbing it with a mixture of bleach and warm water. In the kitchen I occupied many hours cleaning the encrusted appliances. In addition, all of the cupboards and walls throughout the entire unit had to be scoured be-

fore they could be re-painted. I cleaned the fireplace surround and then replaced the broken door glass. In all I
would estimate that the clean-up project cost me at least a
thousand dollars plus many, many hours of my own labor.

A few weeks later I received a telephone call from
the couple who had left the mess. They actually had the un-
adulterated gall to ask when they could expect to receive a
refund of their $300 damage deposit! Needless to say, the
request was pointedly refused and, accompanying the re-
fusal, I gave them a bombastic but free-of-charge lecture on
the proper care and maintenance of rental units.

The last tenant that occupied the mother-in-law
apartment before I sold the house also attended Northwood
Institute. She was a cute and tiny foreign student from Bei-
jing, China. After carefully examining her credentials—
which were in perfect order—I gladly offered her a rental
contract to sign. I was further encouraged about her as a potential renter when she proceeded to question me very carefully about the married couple that rented the larger unit in
the house. She was particularly concerned that they were
quiet and would not have parties because she needed to
spend her time studying. I felt that was a reasonable request
and assured her that she had no worries concerning that issue.

When the new renter had been living in the apartment for a couple of months, I received a telephone call
from her. She already had a complaint about the other tenants. It seemed that they had begun using a small corner of
the common part of the basement for setting up their dart

game. The girl in the smaller apartment was very upset because she felt that they were taking over the common areas and she wanted the dart board removed immediately. After conferring with all three of the tenants together at the house, I concluded that there was no problem for her. She had not been using that area anyway and there were plenty of other spaces available which she could use if she so desired. She wasn't happy with my decision in favor of the other tenants and proceeded to tell me so. I had the distinct impression that she was jealous of them because of their larger apartment and simply wanted to cause difficulties.

The next time I heard from the Chinese student she had yet another complaint. That time she was concerned about the flood light on the front of the garage. Because it illuminated the common driveway, it was controlled by a switch in each of the two apartments and she demanded to know on whose electric bill the cost for it appeared. I didn't know the answer to her question but, felt it was an extremely petty concern. After investigation, I learned that the cost was on the other tenants' bill. Thus, as per usual, she was complaining over nothing. Since she had introduced the issue, I was tempted to insist that she pay for a part of the flood light's costs, but decided not to do so.

Somewhat later I went by the house on one of my usual drive-by inspections and noticed that there was some damage to the overhead door on the girl's side of the shared garage. I called her to ask what happened. She said that she had accidentally hit the metal door with her car. After going to the house and viewing the damage more closely, I told her that I would have it repaired and would send her the bill. She then informed me that her boyfriend was going to mend the dents in the door. Following that there was a heated argument where I insisted that I would have the repair work done professionally and her boyfriend should not attempt it. She, of course, objected strenuously. During the resulting brouhaha the renter, who was only about four feet 2 inches tall and weighed perhaps ninety-eight pounds, threatened me with bodily harm. Eventually I won that round and the boyfriend did not repair the door. Later it was discovered that an entire new door had to be installed in place of the original. After that project was completed, as promised, I presented the tenant with the bill. Grudgingly, and with much ill grace, she did eventually pay it.

By the time all of the above events had transpired, I was so irritated and frustrated with the Asian tenant that I was eager for her lease to expire. During our short association she displayed more troublesome nature than had any of the others from my long list of renters through the years. In fact I did eventually release her from the contract nearly three months early when her college semester came to an end. She was making plans to return to China and I thought that would be a perfect solution for all concerned. I was both relieved and happy to see the last of her.

It is a mystery to me why the mother-in-law apartment seemed to attract the very worst of tenants but that was the case during most of the years it belonged to me. Apparently that is one of life's little conundrums for which there is no obvious or ready answer.

MOTHER-IN-LAW APARTMENT
MIDLAND, MICHIGAN
1989

FRONT ELEVATION

LIVING ROOM

BATHROOM

KITCHEN

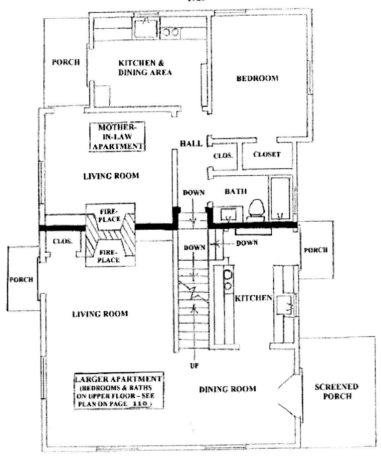

MOTHER-IN-LAW APARTMENT
MIDLAND, MICHIGAN
1989

Chapter Fourteen

The Hundred Year Flood

One overcast dreary September day in the fall of 1986 when I was living in Midland, Michigan, the skies opened up and it began to rain. During the next two days somewhere between ten and fourteen inches of precipitation fell on an area about sixty miles wide from north to south across the central part of the Lower Peninsula of the state. On and off for the next twenty days the downpour continued, blanketing the region with more rainfall than most of its residents had ever experienced in their lifetimes. The resulting deluge, usually referred to as "The Hundred Year Flood", caused between four hundred and five hundred million dollars worth of damage in that part of the state.

Roughly a third of the devastation occurred to farm crops in the Saginaw Valley which includes Midland, Tuscola, Bay and Saginaw counties. September is the middle of the area's harvest season and most of the crops were destroyed in the fields before they could be collected and processed. Damage to thousands of homes in the region accounted for another large part of the cost of that flood. The Chippewa River flows into the larger Tittabawassee River in downtown Midland but, before they meet they cross a big area of river flats. Much of the flats area was flooded when the rivers overflowed their banks and inundated hundreds of homes there. The waters of the Tittabawassee River rose nearly ten feet *above* what was usually considered the flood stage level.

Other factors, besides the rivers over spilling their banks, caused extensive damage to homes in the somewhat higher elevations on the east side of Midland. Because the rainfall came down faster than it could flow away, the soils in parts of the city were saturated with water. As pressures increased, the water forced its way into the foundations and basements where it eroded and sometimes undermined them. In addition, the sewers were overloaded with the excess water; consequently, a contaminated mixture of sewage and rain water often rose through the drains into basement areas. In the local newspapers, city officials published severe warnings to the residents not to re-use the sewage encrusted furniture and other things taken from basements and to carefully dispose of them immediately. For the next month tons of contaminated items lined the streets in that part of the city waiting to be trucked to the disposal grounds by the city's overburdened trash haulers—a sorry sight for a normally tidy and up-scale city.

At that time I owned three houses in Midland, one was my own residence on Sinclair Street, another was a small rental house which was currently occupied by a tenant and the third was a cement block house on Dauer Street that I had recently purchased. Just that month I had begun the clean-up process prior to remodeling the latter house.

Fortunately the flood did very little damage to any of my houses. Some seepage occurred in the basement family room of the house on Sinclair but it was merely uncontaminated ground water. I moved all the furniture up to the first floor for the duration of the flooding and then used my wet/dry utility vacuum to suck up the water. The indoor/outdoor carpet covering the family room floor withstood both the flood and clean-up and was unharmed. The rental house on Montrose Street suffered even less than my own residence. Some ground water seepage occurred there as well, but the sump-pump I had installed in a catch-basin removed it before any damage resulted. Previously I had built an eight inch high platform in the Michigan-style basement in order to keep the furnace, water heater and the tenant's washer and dryer above the cement floor. Because of that platform, the seepage water never touched any of those appliances. The house that I had newly purchased on Dauer Street was a one-level home built on a cement slab so there was no basement to cause any problems. That house was in an area of the city where there was no actual flooding and, even though the surrounding soil was water-drenched, none entered the house.

Currently I was a member of a local rental owner's association called Landlords and Ladies, and at our meetings I heard horror story after horror story of the destruction caused by the flood waters. Some of the rental units belonging to the members were so badly damaged that they abandoned them and went out of the rental business completely. Others were forced to undergo the expense of temporarily housing the tenants in motels while their rental units were being repaired. In general, it was not a good time to be a landlord.

Though the Hundred Year Flood cost me only a small extra expense and some minor problems, I later learned that I had barely escaped a much worse fate. The tragic saga about what happened to a residence which I had previously owned was not a pretty one. I refer to the house on East Campbell Court that I had sold prior to moving to the Sinclair Street house. (See the chapter titled "The Debacle with a Happy Ending"). In that home, besides putting in a swimming pool, I had done extensive remodeling in the previously unfinished basement. I built stud walls in half of the area and divided a large part of it into a bedroom, a family room and a bathroom. I spent a great deal of time, effort and money on the remodel and when I sold the house, the basement was much like a self-contained apartment.

Because of the September rains and subsequent flooding, the ground water next to the house exerted enough pressure on the south basement wall that it collapsed into both the family room and bathroom I had built there. Actually I never saw the horrendous mess that the flooding created but it was described to me in minute detail. My own imagination filled in any blanks that were left. Tons of mud pushed broken cement blocks from the ruined basement wall through the stud walls and destroyed them completely. The gelatinous debris covered the south part of the basement to a depth of approximately two feet. It demolished the bathroom fixtures and damaged the walls, carpeting and furniture in the bedroom and family room. The furnace, the water heater, the washer and the dryer were destroyed by the unrelenting ooze. I can well imagine that the work involved in the basement clean-up process was nothing short of colossal.

Devastation was not limited only to the basement, though it was by far worse there than in other areas. When the south foundation wall gave way, part of the support for the floor joists in the bedrooms on the first floor went with it. The resultant sagging caused structural damage to the framework of the house and, because of that, much of the plaster cracked. The costly repair work involved jacking up the south part of the structure, re-building the cement block basement wall and replacing the damaged framing members, re-plastering walls in the first floor bedrooms and finally repairing the ruined exterior siding.

Mere words cannot express the strong emotions and sense of relief I experienced when I heard the sad tale of the unfortunate house on Campbell Court. Only a slight twist of fate saved me from being the luckless owner who was forced to do all of the expensive and time consuming repair work described above. Even today, twenty-two years after the Hundred Year Flood in Michigan, I tend to break out into a nervous sweat when I ponder what a close call it was for me.

That near miss, though, did not end my renovating fervor. After the great flood episode I spent nearly a year completely remodeling the house on Dauer Street. Three months after it was finished and rented to tenants, I bought a duplex on Hines Street. It took nearly a year and a half to renovate both of its units. If you come away from reading this little volume having learned only one fact, it probably would be that it is nearly impossible to deter a true-blue re-modeler from whatever renovation path he has chosen.

Chapter Fifteen

With Money in the Bank, Why Borrow?

Remodeling costs money. Even if the renovator does the work himself, he still must buy building supplies and the necessary tools to do the project properly. My teacher's salary did not provide much extra money for all of the building and remodeling projects I undertook through the years; therefore I needed to seek additional funding sources to pay for them.

Fortunately I was able to use my savings to pay for much of the first full-house remodeling project at the house on Montrose Street. In addition, some of the expenses came from my regular salary while the renovations were underway. I had purchased the house from the former owner on a land contract with an unusually small monthly payment of $75.00 so that, too, was a help.

The house on Dauer Street was my second full-house remodel and by the time I purchased it, my savings were largely depleted. I figured that I would likely require

about $10,000 of additional money to bring the house to the
point where I could rent it to tenants. The teachers' credit
union, to which I belonged, had an upper limit of $2,000 on
its loans; consequently I had to look elsewhere for the
money I required.

It seemed prudent to investigate the possibility of a
bank loan. However, what I learned about banks and their
policies was a real surprise to me. I began by making an appointment with a representative at the same bank which held
the mortgage for my own residence as well the one on the
house I was planning to remodel. I reasoned that the institution already knew my financial history and it seemed the
perfect choice. I explained the entire situation to the bank
official and he was very happy to oblige. He indicated that
his institution had plenty of money to loan. Also, when the
bank officer mentioned that the loan would require backing
by some sort of collateral, it seemed logical to me. That,
however, was where logic ended in my estimation. He then
asked if I had a bank savings account in the amount of the
$10,000 which could be used for collateral. I was astounded
with his question and answered it with an incredulous question of my own. "With money in the bank, why borrow?"
The illogic of that situation did not seem to occur to the loan
officer at all and he mumbled some sort of reply which
made utterly no sense to me. We looked at one another with
blank expressions and our negotiations seemed to be at an
impasse.

In an attempt to break the stalemate, I suggested that perhaps the $10,000 could be added to the amount I already had borrowed on the house I wished to remodel. When the loan officer checked the mortgage papers to find the appraised valuation of the house, he agreed that would to be a solution to the problem. He then started the necessary paper work. Before we signed the official documents, however, the officer had one more stipulation that also astonished me. He said that the money would only be dispersed to me as I completed the various parts of the renovation. In order for the funds to be released, I would have to produce before and after photos of the remodeling progress. That really bothered me.

In essence, I would be paying monthly payments, plus interest, on money that the bank was still holding until, in its imperious wisdom, it decided to transfer the funds to me. It also meant that the bank probably would be earning additional interest on the money by lending it to other customers at the same time. The loan officer saw nothing strange about the bank's practice and could not understand my objection to the institution's obvious practice of "double dipping."

Later I learned that particular bank had one additional advantage in its dealings with landlords like me. In the entire city of Midland, it was the only institution which would loan *any* money on rental properties. In case we as landlords did not agree with the bank policies, there simply was no other place to turn for needed funds. Therefore it held a virtual monopoly over our ability to borrow on our rental properties. Little wonder that the institution was so overbearing in its practices. Seeing no available alternative, I reluctantly agreed to what I thought were cavalier and audacious loan requirements.

Over the next five or six years I had occasion to gain additional insights into the lending institution's haughty attitudes toward its customers. Here I would like to add a side note about my personal dealings with the bank. As mentioned previously, it held the mortgage for the rental house on Dauer Street in addition to the one on my own residence. From the onset of that mortgage I had added an extra amount, usually three hundred to five hundred dollars, each month in order to pay the loan off faster than the contract stipulated. (Eventually the fifteen year mortgage was paid in full before eight years had elapsed.) Also my payments on all of the loans for the rental units were paid in full and on time. Naively I felt that a payment history of that sort would automatically put me into some sort of preferred group among the bank's customers. Such was not the case.

Each time I bought another house to remodel for use later as a rental, I was subjected to the exact same insulting financial scrutiny which I had undergone during the very first loan application. It was as if they had never heard of me previously. Invariably the officials acted as though I were an itinerant, unemployed vagrant who dared display the brazen gall to waste their valuable time by applying for a loan. I came away from those meetings feeling humiliated, exasperated and maligned. Meanwhile, of course the institution was reaping thousands of dollars in interest on my loans each month, but it lacked the common courtesy to treat me as a valuable customer. Ironically, considering the negative attitudes of the bank officials, I was never turned down for a loan. Obviously, in spite of their ultra conservative lending policies, they recognized profitable ventures when they saw them.

It was especially heartwarming for me when I sold all of my houses, at a sizeable profit I might add, just prior to moving from Michigan to New Mexico. What made it even more pleasurable was that I was able to pay the bank in full for all of the loans on the rental properties. I was gleefully elated over the fact that the bank would no longer have me to kick around emotionally at the same time it was making huge monthly profits from me. "Take that, you arrogant snobs!" I exulted to myself.

As I write this manuscript it is early in the year 2009. Most lending institutions during the past year—particularly those making housing loans—have seen the most serious financial decline since the Great Depression of the early 1930s. Bankruptcies and home foreclosures abound across the entire nation. In fact, the predicament is the most serious experienced during the past seventy years and has caused the banks to plead for and eventually receive huge federal government bailouts. Such action is necessary to forestall their going under financially. I am mystified that such a situation could happen considering my previous dealings with banks and their ultra conservative loan practices. Eventually it occurred to me that apparently the entire lending industry has gone through a total metamorphosis during the fifteen years since I last borrowed money for a house. Loan policies obviously have been liberalized to a dangerous point in order for the institution to end up in its present day plight.

Hindsight, which in my opinion is usually suspect, tells me that had the lenders chosen a middle ground somewhere between their former super conservative actions and the current foolish liberality, perhaps the financial crisis could have been averted. I'm still having a bit of a problem feeling very sorry for the bankers and their dilemma. Ironically though, now my tax money is helping bail them out of their self caused quagmire.

Chapter Sixteen

Why Renovate a Newly-Built House?

When a homeowner makes changes in a house that he has only recently built, logic would seem to tell us that he is wasting his time. One would think that if the owner had spent more time in the planning process then there would be little or no reason for making changes after the house was completed. To me that is reasonable thinking, but I have found that it simply doesn't work that way in the real world. No matter how carefully a house is planned, there always seem to be alterations or improvements that can be made after construction. Living spaces just don't translate exactly the way they should from house plans to the three dimensions of the structure itself. Additionally, one never knows for certain exactly how a space will work for him until he has lived in it for a period of time.

There is another problem which sometimes causes the need for changes. My present home in Albuquerque is a good case in point. Six months before I moved here in 1997,

I signed the papers to have the house built. But, prior to do-ing that, I carefully studied the floor plan and made frequent visits to one of the model houses that had been built from that same plan. I was very familiar with the house both in-side and out and from my observations, I already realized that there were several things that I wanted changed. Surely I could have insisted that the builder make those alterations, but I'm afraid that it would have cost me dearly. Also my renovating juices were flowing at the time and I was very eager to personally take hammer and saw in hand. So, even before I was completely unpacked, I began remodeling. Then later, after I had lived in the house for a time, I became aware of other needed changes.

One of the first alterations I envisioned concerned the master bedroom walk-in closet. It was a good sized stor-age area—about six by nine feet—but the layout did not take full advantage of all that space. The closet had only a single rod for hanging clothing with a shelf above it on each of three sides in the room. The remaining wall was blank. The closet, like all the other rooms in the house, had a ceil-ing that was ten feet high. Because of the availability of all that headroom, I decided to more than double the closet's storage capabilities.

Closet organization kits are readily available but usually come at a high cost, so instead of purchasing one, I decided to design and construct my own. I built a second set of shelves and rods on the three walls which already were being used. That meant that I had to remove the existing ones and raise them up to a higher level in order to make room for the new shelves and rods at the lower level. Additionally, on the unused fourth wall I devised and built racks for neckties and belts, put in hooks to hang bathrobes, built shelves for extra linens and even added a drawer unit for folded shirts and underwear. In that way I was able to use all the available square feet in the space for storage.

Another of my immediate changes to my newly-built house involved the closet of the smaller front bedroom which I planned to use as a music room. When finished it eventually would contain a television set, a VCR, a DVD player, a hide-a-bed for overnight guests and several comfortable chairs for watching television, videos or listening to recordings. The room had a closet with only a single rod and shelf. I removed those and built floor-to-ceiling, wall-to-wall shelves for storing videos and DVDs. In one lower corner of the closet, I left room enough to include a three foot long clothing rod for hanging out-of-season jackets and suits.

A third room that was changed almost immediately after I moved in was the laundry room. Originally, when I bought the house, there was a hook-up for a washer and a dryer in that space but *nothing* else. There were no cupboards or even any shelves for storing laundry supplies like soap, bleach, an iron or any of the many other items connected with laundering. My solution for the problem was to install ready-made cupboards above the washer and dryer and add a taller cupboard unit beside them that extended nearly from floor to ceiling. In the garage I added a work bench, cupboards and a variety of shelving for seasonal items. All of the additional storage units in the walk-in closet, the music room, the laundry room and the garage have seen constant use during the eleven plus years that I have lived here. The interior of the entire house is more comfortable and livable because I was unsatisfied with it as the builder left it and decided to make some immediate changes.

During the past eleven years I have made a number of additional modifications to the house. On the exterior I added more electrical fixtures to better light the main entrance and the garage doors and also added another electrical outlet on the front courtyard wall. That new outlet now allows me to use my yard vacuum on all areas of the property.

At the rear of the house sliding glass doors give access from the living room to a cement patio. There I built what is called a "*portal.*" *Portal* is a Spanish word meaning "porch" but it is a bit different from porches in the Midwest where I was reared. The *portal* is made of "*vigas*" and "*latillias*" that form an open framework for supporting the vines which I planted there. Those vines, after growing for more than eight years, now shade the patio and protect the sliding glass doors from the direct sun rays from the south.

Inside the front courtyard wall, I built an L-shaped "*banco,*" or "bench" with a round fire pit in front and added colored cement paving stones atop the dirt floor. I left room for plantings around the inside of the wall and in one corner added a three-tiered water feature that splashes gently and provides sensory stimulation. Now the courtyard is a delightful and private area that affords a quiet ambience for gatherings large and small.

The home's interior, too, has undergone a few changes through the years. One example is that I added a beam supported by carved corbels above the breakfast bar. That bar divides the living room from the kitchen. The added beam tends to stop the eye at that point and consequently one is not as much aware that the opening leads directly into the kitchen. The beam is placed at an eight foot height, thus it leaves two feet between it and the ceiling for the placement of decorative objects. In addition the new beam supports two hanging lights that provide illumination for the breakfast bar.

My appetite for renovation seems never to be totally satisfied. Just recently I completed yet another building project in the living room of the house. There is a large entrance foyer leading off the living room and its opening is as high as the ceiling and as wide as the foyer itself. There, between the two rooms, I installed another beam, similar to the one I placed over the breakfast bar, at the same eight foot level. It is supported at either end by carved decorative posts and corbels. The completed alteration accomplished my purpose of providing a more attractive transition between the foyer and the living room. In addition the columns and beam further add to the traditional Southwestern architectural style of the house.

I am fully confident that additional changes to the house will occur to me as the years go by. What they entail, whether complicated or simple, I am unable to predict at the present time. I only know for certain that they *will* occur. I live with the ever present feeling that no house is perfect in its present state; therefore, logically it can benefit from alteration and renovation. And, that is my answer to the question with which this chapter began, "Why renovate a newly-built house?" To me the answer seems patently obvious.

REMODELING A NEWLY-BUILT HOUSE
Albuquerque, New Mexico

Newly Built Portal (1999)

Vine covered Portal (2008)

New Fountain in Courtyard

New Banco & Firepit in Courtyard

REMODELING A
NEWLY-BUILT HOUSE
Albuquerque, New Mexico

New Beam over Breakfast Bar

New Laundry Room Storage

Double rods in Master Closet

New Storage in Garage

Video Storage in Music Room

REMODELING A NEWLY-BUILT HOUSE
Albuquerque, New Mexico

FOYER BEFORE

FOYER AFTER

Chapter Seventeen

Invading Animals

Probably anyone who does even a small amount of renovating older houses has animal stories he could tell. I am no exception to the rule and what follows are only a few of the incidents involving a variety of critters which I encountered in my remodeling projects. Like humans, animals need shelter from the elements and they employ a great deal of ingenuity in finding it. Many of the renovations I took on were older houses, some of which had not been occupied for several years. An abandoned house, of course, presents an open invitation for wild creatures to move in. That is akin to a family receiving a coupon granting them free rent in a luxury apartment—an offer which is most difficult to refuse. Critters from the wild, however, do not only search for empty houses when seeking shelter; they also are very willing to jointly occupy a residence and generally are much more willing to do so than their human housemates.

In the late summer of 1986 I purchased a house on Dauer Street in Midland, Michigan. I had recently retired after thirty-one years of teaching and planned to spend most of the next year or so refurbishing the house before renting it to tenants. The residence was a one-story cinder-block house, approximately 1,400 square feet in size, set on a cement slab. The previous owners had abandoned the house after they lost it in an earlier bank foreclosure. The forlorn dwelling sat empty of occupants for a time but, after some of its windows were broken by neighborhood youngsters, a flock of birds moved in and set up house-keeping. They built nests throughout the house, scattered all manner of droppings, food scraps and feathers across the floors and several of them even died there as evidenced by the skeletal remains which I discovered.

After buying the house, one of the first items on my agenda was to dispossess the feathered tenants. That took some doing as they were firmly ensconced and rather unwilling to move out of their cozy habitat. Eventually I won out through steadfast perseverance. To make my claim permanent I repaired the broken windows and sealed all of the various cracks I found in the structure. It is astounding to me how small an opening is required to give critters free and easy access to a building.

Once the birds were forced out, I spent about eleven months remodeling the Dauer Street house. I added a half bath, rebuilt the kitchen cupboards and added new butcher block countertops. I put in a separate laundry room, added new closets in two of the three bedrooms, removed some of the windows, added or replaced others and, finally, carpeted throughout. Outside I renovated the carport, added a lawn equipment storage area, re-seeded the lawn and, lastly, I painted the house. For the next ten years that house was one of my best rentals. It never remained empty for very long before a new tenant moved in.

Shortly after I put the residence up for sale before my move to New Mexico, I had another confrontation with a critter in that particular rental house. About a month after the "for sale" sign went up, the real estate agent located prospective buyers and following some haggling over the conditions of the sale, we came to an agreement for the purchase. One of the contract's provisions was that the final closing on the house would be subject to its passing a building inspection. I readily agreed to that proviso because it is a normal part of most purchase agreements and also I knew that the house was in good condition. Usually I try to accompany the inspectors when they go through my houses but, for some reason I was absent for that particular one. After it was completed, the inspector called to say that he found a surprise in the attic above the main part of the house. He went on to say that he had found a dead raccoon there and he thought it should be removed before the prospective owners bought the home.

It wasn't until I crawled up into the tiny attic space to see for myself, that I learned what had occurred. Apparently the raccoon, while seeking a warm place to live, climbed down an empty flue in the fireplace chimney. Someone had covered the flue's opening in the attic with wire mesh. The raccoon shoved part of the mesh aside but, when he attempted to pass through, the wires snagged him and he could go no further. I don't know how long he struggled against the restraints that held him prisoner but, it was tragically obvious that he had starved to death there in the clutches of the wire mesh. When I encountered the creature, his eyes gaped wide-open in terror and his mouth grimaced in the rictus that accompanied an agonizingly slow demise. What a horrible way to die!

My task of removing the raccoon from his unintended final confinement was not very pleasant either. To help me with the odious job, I gathered together a pair of leather work gloves, a heavy plastic lawn bag and a small garden rake. Using the rake I levered the raccoon's body loose from the claws of the wire mesh. He fell to the floor creating a cloud of dust making the eerie space even darker. All I was aware of were those staring eyes and gawking mouth so haunting to look at in the dimly lit, cramped space of the attic. As quickly as possible, I concealed him in the lawn bag. Nonetheless vivid mental pictures of what I saw still spook me even today. The remains of the unfortunate raccoon now lie in a small grave which I dug in the back yard.

In order to prevent other animals from attempting the same route into the house in the future, I made a few changes up on the roof. I clamped a heavy wire mesh across the two flues which emerged from the chimney, thus making certain that the new buyers would not have to go through the same experience I had faced with the dead raccoon.

The rental house on Hines Street in Midland was the scene of yet another confrontation with critters from the wild. I had spent quite a lot of time remodeling the larger of the two apartments in that house and, after it was completed, I rented it to two single ladies. They seemed very pleased with the unit since it was large, in excellent condition and especially because it included a full bathroom for each of them.

One afternoon, after the new tenants had been living there for a few months, I received a frantic telephone call from one of them. Her voice shook as she hysterically told me what had occurred. Her bedroom, which was on the west side of the second floor, had a built-in drawer unit in one of its side walls where the backs of the drawers extended into the attic area behind. When the tenant opened one of the drawers she saw something dark colored moving among the clothing that was in it. Of course she was alarmed and quickly slammed the drawer closed. She assumed that the moving object was a mouse or a rat and she insisted that I come over to the rental immediately and get rid of it.

On my way out of my house I grabbed a large plastic leaf bag to take along. Experience had shown me that plastic bags always seem to come in handy when dealing with unwanted animals in rental houses. When I arrived, the renter met me at the front door with eyes wide open in terror. She showed me to her bedroom and then stayed just outside the door in the hallway as I assessed the problem. I still did not know for certain what sort of animal it was or how I was going to get rid of it.

After a short deliberation I decided to attempt capturing the creature by using the leaf bag as a cover over the top of the drawer. So I began inching the drawer out and, while doing so, slid the bag across the top of it as it emerged from the opening. The method worked well and when the drawer was fully out of the wall, it was completely covered with the bag. At that point, not only did I still not know *what* was in the drawer, I didn't even know if there was anything in it.

I carried the covered drawer downstairs and out the back door. There I placed it on the porch and removed the bag from the top. When I peered inside I saw a badly frightened but cute little brown bat staring back at me. While bats are not as creepy in my estimation as snakes and rats, they still cannot be numbered among my favorite animals, so I tipped the drawer on its side and the little critter happily flew away.

The brown bat's problem, it seemed, was over but mine was just beginning. I assumed that one bat in the house indicated there were many more—particularly since there was a large empty attic on the third level. The tenants were in a panic and wanted the entire house cleared of the little varmints as soon as possible. I had no idea how to accomplish that, so I called in an expert.

When the exterminator showed up he said there were two ways for him to remove the pesky animals from the house. First, there was the option of sending my tenants to a motel for a couple of weeks and he would shroud the entire house with a balloon-like plastic before releasing poisonous bombs on the inside. Two things about that option were objectionable to me. First, I just wanted the bats to leave, not to be murdered in a poisonous gas attack. After all, the little animals diminish the insect population and thus are beneficial to man. The second problem with that option was the cost. Not only would I have to pay the exterminator's exorbitant fee, but I would have to foot the bill for two motel rooms for a period of several weeks while my tenants could not live in the house.

The other option for removing the bats was a little less expensive—it cost only $800. The plan was much more complicated but the renters could remain in the house while it was underway. The exterminator would drape the entire house (except for the entrances) with a fine wire mesh. That allowed the bats to still find their way out of the house under the shroud. However, when they attempted to re-enter, they were unable to find routes through the mesh, eventually causing them to give up and re-locate elsewhere. By the time the mesh had been in place for two weeks, all the bats had vacated the house and the exterminator removed it and filled each crack of ¼ inch or more in size with steel wool and wood putty. His action ensured that no other bat colony could enter the house to set up housekeeping. In retrospect, it seems impossible that an adult brown bat, which is of comparable size to mouse, except for its wings, was able to crawl through a crack only ¼ inch across. Nonetheless, when all the above had been accomplished, the house on

Hines Street returned to normal and I never heard any more complaints from the renters about bats.

Wild animals continued to be a bone of contention for me after I moved to New Mexico. The only difference was that the critters were of different species than those I encountered in the Midwest. Here is an example. My new house is located on the far western side of Albuquerque and is in an area that formerly had been a scrubby section of the high desert with tumbleweeds, some chamisas, and a few other desert-type plants. One of the workmen who was doing some of the final finish work on the house told me that a year previous to that he had been hunting jackrabbits in that same area.

I hadn't lived in the Southwest more than six months before I saw the first scorpion in the house. That shook me up rather badly because all my life I had heard how deadly poisonous scorpions can be. Immediately I called the city's pest control hot line to learn more about the unwanted visitor. The lady who answered my call first asked the color of the insect. (Though I usually think of them as insects, scorpions instead are called arachnids.) When I indicated that it was a coral color, she explained that, though it was poisonous, it was not deadly. Its sting was about like that of a honey bee. The lady went on to explain that the black scorpions, found in the southwestern part of the state, near Silver City, are much more dangerous.

Over the next few months I probably encountered a half dozen or more additional scorpions inside the house. Apparently it had been built on a nest of them. That prompted me to get in touch with an exterminator company. Since then a man comes each month to spray around the base of the entire house on the outside and then does the same on the inside as well. He also sets traps here and there in secluded spots inside the house and garage. I have found that the critter population has diminished greatly but, upon occasion I still do see a few, including scorpions.

Because this is a desert, several of my nearby neighbors have also seen rattlers in or near their properties, but, fortunately, I have been spared that. However, a tiny green snake was snared by one of the exterminator's traps in the living room. It is the only snake I have seen in the wild while living in Albuquerque. I don't know how it managed to get inside the house or how the snake ended up dying in the trap, but that was where the exterminator found its body.

As previously stated, this chapter could be much longer since I have many, as yet untold, stories about wild critters in and around my remodeling projects. The ones I have already related, though, are good examples of the more interesting of them and should suffice nicely. I would need an entire sequel to this volume in order to tell about all of my confrontations with such creatures as mice, squirrels, lizards, pigeons, mourning doves, sparrows, rabbits, coyotes, centipedes, millipedes, swarms of flies, mosquitoes, bees and hornets, plus the singularly repulsive cockroaches.

Chapter Eighteen

The Emergence of the Mega Stores

When I first began my career in home remodeling, the business of selling building products differed greatly from what it is today. In those times when renovators and remodelers went shopping for the tools, building supplies, and technical information necessary for their projects, they had to shop at many separate and individual businesses. The mega sized home improvement stores which we take for granted today had not as yet come on the scene. There were no nearby establishments like Lowe's and Home Depot available where the renovator could do one-stop shopping for items as varied as a length of door trim to plants for their exterior landscaping.

Like every other renovator, I went to an electrical store if I needed lighting supplies; when I required 2 x 4s, plywood and wood trim I sought out a lumber yard; if I wanted to do some painting I bought the paint and brushes at a paint store; in case I needed nails, screws, hinges or bolts I made my way to a hardware store. Because of that situation, dyed in the wool renovators, like me, were required to make themselves familiar with a large number of different places of business as well as the sales personnel operating those establishments. In addition, we were forced to waste valuable time, money for gasoline, and we experienced costly wear and tear on our vehicles while doing our shopping at stores often widely separated from one another.

Hauling building materials from the suppliers to the site where I was doing the renovating sometimes led to problems and situations that were difficult and occasionally even dangerous. Let me digress here to relate an experience I had while transporting lumber for a deck I was building at the back side of my house in Midland, Michigan. Because I had been shopping for bargains, I ended up purchasing the materials at a lumber yard some twenty miles away in Mount Pleasant. Considering what happened later, that was probably a mistake on my part. In fact it *definitely* was a mistake that could have had dire consequences.

For transporting the lumber I was using a light utility trailer that I hauled behind my car. The trailer's back, front and sides were made of 1x 4 boards and it was about eight or nine feet in length from front to rear. The lumber purchased that day consisted of twelve foot long 2 x 6 planks. Since the planks were longer than the trailer I tied them at an angle from the floor at the front and then across the top of the trailer's back side. That left a little more than three feet sticking out behind. I attached a red flag on the end of the lumber and started out on the twenty mile trip to Midland.

When I was about five miles along the way, I drove over a bump in the highway which caused the lumber to bounce. It landed sharply on the rear part of the trailer and crushed the top 1 x 4 supporting it. That forced the back of the trailer to go down sharply, which raised the tongue up, and in doing that, unhitched it from the car! I recall looking with alarm in the rear view mirror as the trailer followed the car for a short time but then, horror of horrors, turned to the left into the oncoming traffic lane. Fortunately there were no cars on that particular stretch of the highway so the trailer, with the lumber still on board, careened across the other lane in a big arc and eventually came to a stop, facing the opposite direction, in a shallow ditch at the roadside.

When my frazzled nerves had settled down a bit, I collected myself and decided upon a course of action. I called a friend with a pickup truck who came to my rescue. We loaded the lumber on his vehicle and he drove to Midland. Surprisingly, except for the one broken 1 x 4, the trailer was undamaged, so once more I hitched it to my car and I, too, headed for Midland. As one can well imagine, soon after that I sold the trailer and bought my first pickup truck to be used for hauling building supplies.

That close call probably would never have happened if Midland had a Home Depot or a Lowe's at the time. My experience has shown me that those two businesses usually have the lowest prices available; therefore comparison shopping for building supplies generally is no longer necessary.

During the early 1970s I saw the first precursor to what would later become the home building mega stores. I lived in Saginaw, Michigan at the time and heard about the opening of the first Wickes Lumber Company stores in the area. Prior to that I had always associated Wickes Company only with ship building, probably because of the company's operations in nearby Bay City, where they manufactured boilers for ocean-going vessels. While doing the research for this book, however, I learned that Wickes already had a long history in lumber as well. In fact, when the company was first formed that was its primary product, but during World War II, lumber took a back seat to boilers and graphite products.

When the first Wickes store opened in Saginaw I was quick to investigate because of all the advertising hoopla that had preceded it about "a NEW type of business." My reaction upon first entering the establishment was almost as a child on his first visit to a candy emporium. In the large showrooms I found not only the usual building items such as lumber, milled products, tools, nails and screws, but also ready-made cupboards, carpeting, counter tops, electrical and plumbing supplies and an entire range of other items not usually associated with lumber yards up until that time. Enthralled, I wandered from one fascinating display to another, up and down the crowded aisles for hours at a time. As I feasted my eyes on all that was before me, I realized that for the first time a builder, without stepping outside of that one store, actually could order nearly all the items he needed to build a complete house.

The rise of a retail business called Builder's Square was the next step I was aware of in the emergence of the present-day mega building supply stores. The first Builder's Square I visited was also near Saginaw and to me its size was astounding. It appeared to be as large as several football fields placed side by side. That enormous square footage gave it a distinct advantage over the Wickes stores. Where Wickes usually could supply the builder with only one brand of a certain type of material, Builder's Square could display several brands at a variety of different pricing levels. For a small-scale renovator like me, that was real progress for it suited my needs exactly. When I made improvements in my own home, for example, I normally used top-of-the-line products, but when remodeling rental houses, I often used middle-grade materials. My aim, of course, was to save money, but also I had an aversion to subjecting expensive materials to possible misuse by irresponsible or uncaring tenants.

Recently I visited a Lowe's Home Building Store to order blinds for my kitchen window and sliding doors. I measured the openings carefully before leaving home and presented the measurements to the person in charge of the blinds department. On that visit I probably viewed samples of at least twenty different styles of blinds. Some were wooden and others were plastic. A few of the examples were extremely expensive but most were moderate to inexpensive in price. There were samples of blinds in every size and color imaginable. The clerk who waited on me asked question after question about the exact type of blind I desired. Often I was at a loss concerning how to answer, as she glibly referred to variations in blinds that I had never thought about or heard of previously—and all of them available at Lowe's. In addition, I could have the blinds delivered and professionally installed or I could pick them up at the store and do the installation myself. The possibilities seemed endless.

That was just one example of the valuable types of services which the mega home building stores such as Lowe's and Home Depot now provide the serious home renovator or remodeler. What a contrast that story is from the conditions which existed fifty plus years ago when I undertook my first baby steps in renovating and remodeling.

Epilogue

Clearly, it was never my intention to become a landlord. That phase of my life occurred simply as a result of my
love of renovating and remodeling. In 1981 I bought a house
with the idea of spending the next year or so renovating the
place inside and out. That was merely because I was interested in seeing what I could make of the forlorn and decrepit
structure. Unfortunately, when the project was completed I
felt that the house had become such an integral part of me,
that I just couldn't put it on the market as had been my
original plan. Eventually I talked myself into attempting a
trial run at renting the house to tenants. Thus, through de-
fault, my new career of landlord was launched.

That first experience was so pleasant and gratifying
that it encouraged me to continue in the role of landlord.
Thus, every other year for approximately the next ten years,
I added to my stable of rental units until I owned a total of
five. In each case I bought a "junker" type of house and
worked on it until I was satisfied with its condition and then
looked for a tenant to occupy it. Throughout the decade and

a half between 1982 and 1997 I rented to thirty-seven different tenants. My rental business experiences taught me
that often the relationship between tenant and landlord can
be a virtual game with a variety of players on both sides of
the gaming field.

Landlords are not all the same. They run the gamut
from conscientious to *laissez-faire*. Some are in the business
merely to make a quick profit, and maintain their properties
only to the bare extent necessary to keep them filled with
tenants. They exhibit little or no pride in ownership, and
consequently their rentals often display that lack of personal
attention. The second type of rental owner treats the units
with care and maintains them in a relatively conscientious
manner. A third type of landlord looks upon the rentals in
the same way that he does his own private residence. He
takes care of all maintenance and repair work immediately
and insists that his tenants treat the units with respect and
consideration. I must confess to being the latter type of landlord—perhaps at times, overly so.

As with landlords, I would classify my thirty-seven
tenants in three main categories. First, were those who lived
in the houses or the apartments as if in their own homes.
Cleaning up after them was very simple—in fact an almost
nonexistent job. The second group of tenants caused no real
damage, but their vacated dwellings showed signs of having
been lived in. The clean-up task usually involved cleaning
the carpets, painting throughout, washing the windows and
cleaning the bathroom fixtures, in addition to scrubbing the
cupboards and appliances in the kitchen. The third category

treated their living quarters as if they were flop houses and seemed bent on destroying them. They normally left the rental looking like a pig sty. Cleaning up after a category three tenant could be daunting. Often, carpets had to be replaced and broken fixtures needed repair or replacement. Sometimes it was even necessary to patch the plaster throughout the unit before the walls could be re-painted. In addition, it was usually necessary to buy new curtains, window shades and draperies and occasionally the windows themselves had to be re-glazed.

Fortunately the middle group made up the largest percentage of the thirty-seven tenants with whom I had dealings. There were exceptions, however, on both ends of the scale as indicated by several of the previous chapters. I experienced no resentment about doing the necessary clean-up involved in renting to the sort of tenant who caused only the expected amount of wear and tear on the unit. In fact, I felt that it was at least a part of why they were paying rent in the first place. Therefore it was merely one of the necessary accoutrements to being in the landlord business.

Occasionally I have been asked about my preference in renters—if I felt that men or women were superior. Through the years, I have given that question quite a lot of thought and it is not a simple one to answer. If the query had been, what group made up the very worst of tenants—those whom I would prefer not to have in my rental units—the answer would have been much simpler. I would immediately have replied "college students." That one group of renters, whether male or female, has the ignoble distinction of having been, not only *my* least favorite tenant, but that of nearly every landlord I have ever met. When I belonged to the rental owners association called Landlords and Ladies, our group meetings often evolved into wild discussions during which each of us recounted our never ending headaches with college students as tenants.

If I answered the question about my preferences in tenants today, from across the time span of more than ten years since I sold my last rental, I would separate them according to whether the renters were orderly or slipshod and whether they were conscientious or irresponsible. Using those categories it would be nearly impossible for me to favor either men or women in choosing preferred tenants.

Some of my very best renters were women, as were some of the worst. Mrs. Carris was my first renter and she, with her two daughters, occupied the small house on Montrose Street. Through my experiences with her and her family, she proved to be the epitome of what an ideal tenant should be. The next tenant in that same house, Mrs. Doyle, as it developed, was the exact opposite. She earned the dubious honor of being as bad a tenant as Mrs. Carris was a good one. Both Mrs. Carris and Mrs. Doyle earned the honor of having entire chapters devoted to their actions as renters.

Certain men, too, were exceptional as tenants while others would have to be relegated to the worst category. You will likely recall the chapter about the mother-in-law apartment where I described the unbelievable chaos left by a young man and his live-in girlfriend. The two of them nearly destroyed the small rental unit during their short six-month occupancy.

As an example of how seriously I took my role of watchful landlord, consider the following. Each time I rented a unit to a tenant I insisted on a lease contract which spelled out the terms of the rental agreement. One of the clauses in that contract stated that the apartment or house was to be kept in good condition both inside and out. Another clause allowed me to make surprise inspections of the property if I so desired. I did that upon occasion during the decade and a half that I was in the business and usually the units were in at least a decent state but, as I have already explained, sometimes just the opposite was true.

Still another clause in the lease contract dealt with finances. It spelled out the amounts of damage deposit, the monthly rent and when the due dates were. A number of the worst tenants apparently felt that the due dates for rent payments were merely something toward which to aim, but only if it were convenient. Those tenants seemed oblivious of the fact that I, as the house owner, was required to pay property taxes, make regular mortgage payments, and had numerous other expenses. Expenses that remained constant whether or not the tenants paid their rents on time.

I would be remiss if I left out the following story about two of the finest male tenants with whom I ever had any dealings. During the summer of 1996 I rented my small house on Montrose Street to two men in their early thirties. Their initial damage deposit and all of the following rental payments were submitted on time and for the full amounts.

As with the other units, I made drive-by inspections every once in a while and the house and surroundings were always in perfect order. On one of those passes, however, I noticed that some interesting alterations had been made in the side yard.

A few years prior I had built a post and woven wire fence in that area to divide the front and rear spaces. In order to give easy access between the two areas I added a wooden gate near the house. Obviously the tenants thought the fence appeared somewhat unsightly and, in retrospect, I would have to agree with them. To solve the problem they covered the entire side of the fence facing the street with vertical slatted boards and stained them a dark color to blend with the brown exterior of the house. Then they landscaped along the fence with flowers and other plantings. I thought the entire effect was much more attractive than my original fence had been and applauded the changes. The renters never asked for any reimbursement for their costs and left the improvements in place when they moved out at the end of their contractual time.

Here is an interesting side note about those tenants. During the time that they rented the Montrose Street house, they owned a small used furniture store in downtown Midland. Their business dealt mainly in inexpensive, previously owned items but occasionally they had a few antiques on hand. Both of the owners possessed a real talent for home decorating. Each time I visited the rental house while they lived there I came away impressed with how they had furnished the small unit. Though they used only bargain-basement type, older pieces of furniture and wall décor, they arranged them in a manner which made the place a most attractive residence. One would assume that they had spent a great deal of money for advice from a professional decorator, but such was not the actual case.

I was rather upset when the guys decided to move to Saginaw and consequently did not renew their rental contract at the end of the first year. Good renters, such as they, were hard to come by and were a landlord's dream type of tenant.

During the time I was a landlord, I often thought it would be nice if someone invented a machine that would determine, ahead of time, what sort of tenant a prospective renter would make. I imagined a sort of TID or "Tenant Imaging Device." That machine would have made my job of selecting renters a great deal easier but, of course, it also would have taken much of the adventure out of playing the captivating and intriguing game of "Landlord Versus Tenant."

About The Author

Jerry R. Davis was born in 1932 and grew up in the Thumb Area of Michigan's Lower Peninsula. He earned bachelor and master degrees in history from Michigan State University and Central Michigan University, respectively. Jerry taught history in a number of Michigan junior high schools for thirty-one years prior to retiring from the education field in 1986. The first decade of his retirement he spent volunteering in a hospital, working on his family genealogy and remodeling old houses into rental properties.

In 1997 Jerry moved to Albuquerque, New Mexico and began a new career in the field of writing. Since then he has been a freelance author with articles appearing in several newsletters, *The Good Old Days* magazine and also in the *Posh New Mexico* magazine. *Master of None* is Jerry's fourth book of memoirs. His third memoir, *Leafing Through My Family Tree,* was a finalist in the 2008 New Mexico Book Awards contest.

Jerry is a member of SouthWest Writers, the New Mexico Book Coop and the Writers to Writers Workshop— all organizations of New Mexico authors and centered in Albuquerque.